*Dedicated to
my Mom and Dad,
Dave and Louise Botz,
and to all Vietnam veterans*

ISBN number: 9781463535803

Also by Chris Noel — *Matter of Survival: The War Jane Never Saw*

Contents © 2011 Chris Noel and Kirk Kimball. All rights reserved. No portion of this book may be reproduced without permission, except for review or other promotional purposes. All photos and images © their respective owners.

CHRIS NOEL
CONFESSIONS OF A PIN-UP GIRL

INTRODUCTION BY
NANCY SINATRA

DESIGNER/EDITOR
KIRK KIMBALL

CHRIS NOEL INTERVIEWS **NANCY SINATRA**
FOR HER SHOW "A DATE WITH CHRIS,"
ON ARMED FORCES RADIO, 1965.

INTRODUCTION

What can I say about my old friend Chris? When she asked me to write this introduction, my mind scanned four decades of memories — from Hollywood to Vietnam to Washington, DC. There is a lot to say, but space is limited, dear reader, so I will simply praise Chris, because she doesn't really give herself the credit she deserves.

An unsung fashion icon, Chris Noel helped create '60s pop culture, bringing eyeliner and mini-skirts to the masses: young women who were aching for a change from poodle skirts, and men who were happy to see legs instead of petticoats!

Because of Chrissy's incredible beauty, she can bring light by simply standing there and smiling — but she is also a talented actress and comedienne whose presence on the screen is a joy to behold. Whether on film, television, or in a live setting, her sweetness radiates to each member of the crew, her fellow performers and the audience. You simply can't take your eyes off her, and your heart melts.

There is no way to thank Chris for all she has done for our troops and veterans. Nobody knows how many people she has helped over the years, in the decades since the Vietnam War, but she has never looked for glory or gratitude anyway, so it's a moot point. Unselfish dedication is such a big part of who she is.

Having experienced great personal sorrow herself, Chris knows what it's all about when she comforts a wounded warrior in a hospital or helps a homeless veteran find his place in the world after giving so much of his life away. She is a true hero.

On behalf of our entire generation, Chrissy, thank you for your service to our country. I'm proud to know you.

Nancy Sinatra

P.S. I wish Chris and my dad had dated more, and I hope my kids don't see that picture of me with the cigarette! ;)

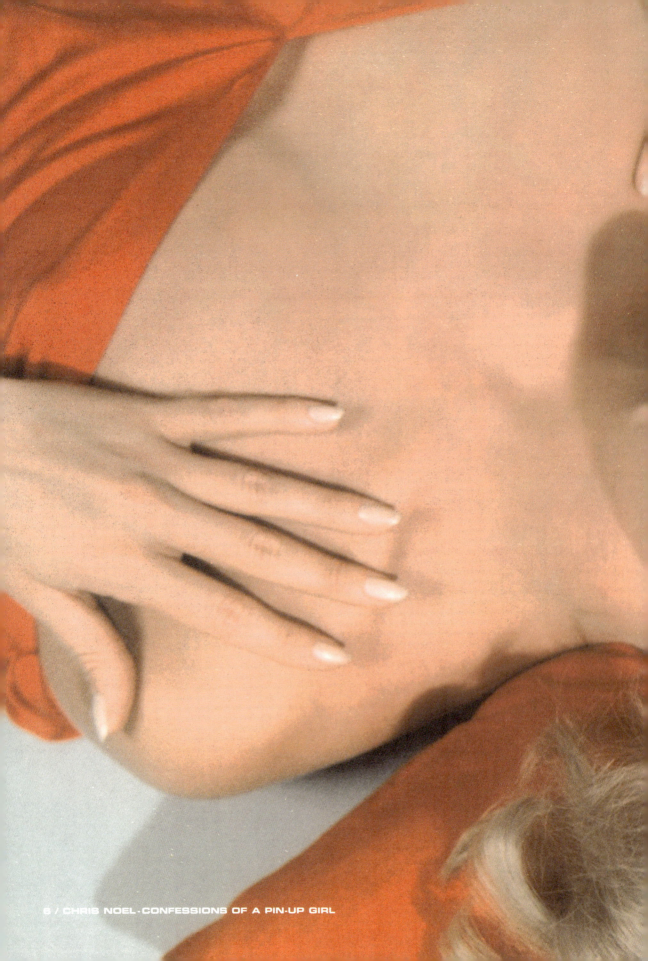

My parents, Dave and Louise

JD Noel

Me at five years old

My sister Pudie and I

PART ONE
Born on the Beach

I WAS BORN ON THE BEACH. To be precise, I was born in a hospital in West Palm Beach, Florida, on July 2, 1947.

My birth name was Sandra Louise Noel. My biological father, J.D. Noel, was a police officer with an eye for women. My mother, Louise, divorced him when I was a child, and remarried a wonderful man named David Botz. I remained Sandee Noel.

When I was a little girl, I'd sit on the beach and read movie magazines by the dozen, devouring everything about Hollywood and movie stars, especially Marilyn Monroe.

I dreamed of becoming famous one day, just like Marilyn — never mind my glasses, bow legs, buck teeth, stage fright, and the fact that in my early teens, I was only about five-foot-five inches tall.

No one knew it at the time, but there were a lot of other kids in my high school who also had dreams of fame, such as George Hamilton, and Burt Reynolds.

I had big dreams, and wanted to do something special with my life. Like many teenage girls, I had fantasies of becoming a famous actress, living a glamorous, exciting life, and dating lots of handsome, wealthy men.

At 17, I began modeling (that's my "resume" on the right — my first pin-up!), and managed to land some high-prestige jobs, like appearing in ads for Kodak film and Miami travel brochures. I decided to open my own modeling school in the Palm Beach Ballet Studio in Lake Park, Florida.

I taught what I had learned to other girls my age, while doing occasional jobs myself, modeling various swimsuits and products, often posing on one of Florida's many beautiful beaches.

Sandee Noel

EYES — BLUE GREEN	SWIM SUIT — 12	BUST — 36
HAIR — BLONDE	GLOVE — 7	WAIST — 24
COMPLEXION — FAIR	HEIGHT — 5' 6"	HIPS — 35
DRESS — 9, 10, 11	WEIGHT — 115	SHOE — 7½ B

Sandee Becomes Chris

ON MY 18TH BIRTHDAY, I decided to leave Florida and relocate in New York City, hoping to make it big.

Shortly after arriving in Manhattan, I went to the Ford Agency and spoke with Eileen Ford, the ultimate modeling power-broker. She directed me to the Foster Ferguson Agency.

For some reason, they wanted me to adopt the stage name of "Liz Barrett" — but I insisted on keeping the name Noel.

"Liz Noel" didn't sound right, so eventually we settled on "Chris." I dyed my hair blonde, and the former Sandee Noel officially became CHRIS NOEL.

As Chris Noel, I posed for several ads and magazine covers. My baton-twirling abilities were put to good use when I became one of the first professional cheerleaders for the New York Giants Football team.

I was thrilled to get paid ten dollars per game. It sounds small, but that was a lot of money for a teenage girl way back in 1962!

Above: Swimsuit ad May 1961, and True Medic Stories, Nov. 1962

Below: Modern Romances, Dec. 1962

Miss Rheingold

Finalists in the "Miss Rheingold" contest were given cards like the one shown above. Winners got their picture on Rheingold Beer for a year.

RHEINGOLD BEER used to print pictures of pretty girls on their cans, and every year they held a nationwide contest to find new "Rheingold Girls."

I was lucky enough to become one of six finalists in the Miss Rheingold Girl contest of 1963. In the end I didn't win, but finalists still received beautiful clothes, use of limousines, and tons of media exposure.

The New York Daily News called me "One of the girls in your future." *The News* added, "Chris has frequently been called another Marilyn Monroe."

Another Marilyn Monroe?!? Oh my God! That was all the encouragement I needed. Maybe I *could* make it as an actress — but at the time, almost all the acting jobs were in California. So I saved my money, and as soon as I had enough, I left New York and headed for Hollywood.

HOLLYWOOD GO GO TEEN ALBUM

MEET

THE GIRLS IN THE WILDEST HOUSE IN TOWN

Kathy Kersh, met Bill on Martian, later dated him and brought him to the house she shares with three other bachelor blondes.

A model and actress, Patricia Olson is also a tenant. The girls share clothes, food, have lots of pets, but don't share their men.

Chris Noel works with Gary Lockwood, but dates Hugh O'Brian, a very steady visitor who generally comes in a tux, while Bill's in levis.

Singer Mary Taylor rounds up the quartette. All the girls aspire to show biz careers, date mostly actors or others in the field.

Bill Bixby gets a kick out of visiting Kathy in the big house up in Coldwater Canyon—the wildest house in town, he says—where she lives with "three other knockouts": Chris Noel, featured in *The Lieutenant*, Pat Olson, a model, and Mary Taylor, a singer.

"Almost any Friday night that place would be a bonanza for autograph hunters because the girls all date people in show business."

"It's real kooky. One guy, maybe Hugh O'Brian, will show up in a tuxedo to pick up Chris. I'll show in dungarees for Kathy; another fellow will be in a business suit for Pat, and still another in sports clothes to take out Mary."

"We'll all sit around and chat while waiting for our dates to get ready and it's like Grand Central Station as people come and go. We never double date."

PART TWO
Hollywood Starlet

IN HOLLYWOOD, I moved into a horrible little hotel on Sunset Boulevard, near Beverly Hills. The place was dreary, so I eventually called a few girlfriends, some of whom had also been Reinhold Girl contestants. We all got together and rented a nice, big house in Coldwater Canyon, in Beverly Hills.

There were four of us living in that house, and we were all in show business. Myself, plus model/actress Patricia Olson; singer Mary Taylor, and Kathy Kersh, then a regular on "My Favorite Martian." Kathy was dating Bill Bixby, the star of "Martian," but she was the only one of us with a steady boyfriend.

There was always something crazy going on at our place — never a dull moment. A 1962 article in "Hollywood Go Go Teen Album" magazine (pictured left) called us "The girls in the wildest house in town."

Famous television producer Aaron Spelling, creator of "Dynasty," "Charlie's Angels" and hundreds of other shows, once said he should have filmed a series in our house. He was right.

Every week one of us had a different romantic entanglement. It was like living in a sitcom! Bill Bixby said it was "like Grand Central Station as people come and go."

At the time, I was dating Hugh O'Brian, although we weren't exclusive. Hugh was the star of the hit TV series Wyatt Earp, and we first met when he was judging the Miss Reingold Girl contest. Hugh is a truly remarkable man. Let me tell you about him.

Polka dots in sunburst effect highlight daring cutouts in one-piece maillot of nylon (Sea B's, $21). The girl it decorates is 23-year-old Chris Noel, a TV actress.

JUNE 10, 1966 **LIFE**

NEWARK SUNDAY NEWS - HOLLYWOOD PAGE

Hugh and Chris add their good cheer to Academy Awards reception gala

Keep your eye on this attractive duo, Hugh O'Brian and Chris Noel, 'cause they just might be meant for each other.

THE NEW YORK POST - MAY 27, 1963

It Happened Last Night
By Earl Wilson

ALL GREAT MEN have their weaknesses—and it took a pretty girl to discover Hugh O'Brian's. Chris Noel, who'll appear with him in "Mr. Roberts," told me what it is: "He likes to have his shoulder blades massaged."

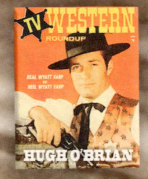

TV WESTERN ROUNDUP
REAL WYATT EARP vs REEL WYATT EARP
HUGH O'BRIAN

18 / CONFESSIONS OF A PIN-UP GIRL by CHRIS NOEL

Heavenly Hugh O'Brian

I FIRST MET Hugh O'Brian when he was a judge of the Miss Reinhold contest. Hugh was a very popular actor at the time. He's appeared in tons of feature films, mostly westerns — but he's probably best known for playing "Wyatt Earp" on TV from 1955 to 1961.

After I moved out to Hollywood, Hugh and I began dating. Hugh was a magnificent, sexy man, and we had a torrid affair. We'd dress up to the nines and go out on the town, clubbing until the wee hours of the night. The gossip columns regularly ran pictures of us out together. The Newark Sunday News Hollywood page captioned a photo of us (shown opposite page, upper left) together at an Academy Awards reception: *"HUGH and CHRIS ... keep your eye on this attractive duo, because they just might be meant for each other!"*

I always had a blast with Hugh. He was so full of life! Pictured left is a photo of him about to throw me into his swimming pool. I still keep in touch with Hugh, and in January 2009 I threw him a huge gala at the Palm Beach Ritz Carlton to celebrate his lifetime of achievement, both in Hollywood, and as one of the youngest Drill Instructors in the WWII Marine Corps. Hugh was deeply moved by this tribute, and I was thrilled to be able to give it to him. Hugh O'Brian, I still love you. *What a wonderful man!*

MR. ROBERTS
Director: Billy Matthews
Play by: Joshua Logan
Based on the novel by:
Thomas Heggen
Date: June 1963
Cast: Hugh O'Brian, Vincent Guardenia, Will Hutchinson, Gary Crabbe, Chris Noel
Trivia: Chris and Will Hutchinson also appeared in "Legal Eagle," an unaired pilot for a television series

Mr. Roberts

THANKS TO HUGH O'BRIAN, I got my first-ever acting job, a role in the stage play "Mr. Roberts," at the Westbury Music Fair on Long Island, New York.

"Mister Roberts" is a 1948 play based on the 1946 Thomas Heggen novel of the same name. It's a comedy set aboard the USS Reluctant, in the South Pacific during WWII.

I was thrilled to be working with Hugh, of course. He had the title role, which was played by Henry Fonda on Broadway and in the movie. Other cast members included Vincent Gardenia, a superb actor who would later appear on "All in the Family," and Gary Crabbe, son of movie serial king Buster Crabbe.

The play had an all-male cast, 28 men, and just one woman, me. I was the only female in the entire show, playing a Navy nurse. The guys couldn't do enough for me. They treated me like a queen, and I have to admit I loved every minute of it.

I had never taken acting lessons, or appeared in school plays. I was too scared of speaking in public to even stand up and read my book reports. Acting still scared me, especially acting on stage, in front of a live audience. But modeling had helped me get over a lot my fears, and my darling Hugh was constantly encouraging me with moral support.

I guess it worked, because during the limited run of this play, I was offered a chance to be in a new TV series, created by Gene Roddenberry.

A KISS FOR LUCK FROM HUGH O'BRIAN

Rehearsing with Randy Kirby.

THE LIEUTENANT
Network: NBC
Cast: Gary Lockwood, Robert Vaughn, Richard Anderson, Chris Noel
Season: One season only, 29 episodes. Chris appears in seven episodes.
- "A Million Miles from Clary" (Episode 1, Aired Sept. 14, 1963)
- "Cool of the Evening" (Episode 2, Aired Sept. 21, 1963)
- "The Proud and the Angry" (Episode 3, aired Sept. 28, 1963
- "Instant Wedding" (Episode 9, Aired Nov. 9, 1963)
- "The Art of Discipline" (Episode 13, Aired Dec. 21, 1963)
- "Between Music and Laughter" (Episode 17, Aired Jan. 25, 1964)
- "Tour of Duty" (Episode 23, Aired March 7, 1964)

Length: 60 minutes, black and white
Trivia: First TV series created by Star Trek's Gene Roddenberry; first series to star the same actress, Chris Noel, as a "Rotating Regular," playing a different character in each episode.

The Lieutenant

BEFORE "STAR TREK," Gene Roddenberry, created a TV series called "The Lieutenant," starring Gary Lockwood as Lt. William Rice, a Marine stationed in Camp Pendleton, in California.

I did two episodes of the show without a contract, then Gene decided he liked what I was bringing to the cast, so he asked me to become a regular — or, as Gene put it, a "roaming regular."

What a brilliant idea! Gene was wonderful man, too. He saw me as a real actress, not just a model who wished she could act.

I played a different character in each of the seven episodes I appeared in — a secretary, a woman Marine, a nightclub singer, a beach bunny, then one of Lt. Rice's many girlfriends, both on *and off* the show. Gary Lockwood and I dated regularly during filming. I thought we had something going, but one night I called him and another woman answered the phone. It was *Dynasty* star Linda Evans.

She told me, "Gary is asleep." I thought, oh well. Guess he's moved on from me!

Even though "The Lieutenant" got good ratings, it was canceled after one season. Gene said it was because the Vietnam War's increasing unpopularity made doing a military show impossible. In the last episode, Gene sent Lt. Rice to Vietnam.

ATTENTION? YES SIR!

A kiss from Gary Lockwood.

Los Angeles Times, October 6, 1963

Here, Chris appears in her "dress uniform," which she wears in a night club scene from episode of the military series on NBC network.

Chris Noel, the heartthrob of NBC's "The Lieutenant," poses on the beach in her "Marine" uniform—a polka dot bikini. Shape up, soldier!

Attention!

● It's too early to tell if NBC's Marine series, "The Lieutenant," will pass inspection come award time, but one of its regular cast members, Chris Noel, has passed inspection by every male viewer. Her role in the series is unique. She portrays a different character in every episode (night club singer, waitress, secretary, etc.). Having Chris around improves the morale of the young Marines. Sort of makes them real gung ho! And it only goes to prove that basic training can't be all bad—if you're a civilian.

The New York Mirror, Sunday, September 8, 1963.

SOLDIER IN THE RAIN
Director: Ralph Nelson
Studio: Allied Artists
Screenplay by: Blake Edwards
Based on novel by: William Goldman
Release date: November 27, 1963
Cast: Steve McQueen, Jackie Gleason, Tuesday Weld, Tony Bill, Tom Poston, Ed Nelson, Adam West, Chris Noel
Music: Henry Mancini
Length: 88 minutes, black and white
Trivia: Released the same week President John F. Kennedy was assassinated.

Soldier in the Rain

AFTER THE LIEUTENANT, I auditioned for a part opposite Steve McQueen, then almost had a heart attack when they called and told me the part was mine.

Soldier in the Rain was a black and white film, a comedy about two military men and their crazy adventures. Steve played the younger man, and Jackie Gleason played his idol. Working with the famous "Great One" was fun, but the best thing about getting this part was the chance to work with Steve McQueen.

By this time, Steve had already starred in *Wanted: Dead or Alive* (1958-1960), and *The Great Escape* (1963), so he was a well-established star. I was a total novice playing her very first role in a Hollywood movie. Jackie Gleason called me "The 1964-model Cinderella — Cinderella with *pizazz!*"

When I first met Steve, I told him that I loved his movies. He seemed genuinely moved. He asked me what I thought about my part in "Soldier in the Rain."

"I'm playing your girlfriend, Frances McCoy. She's a nymphomaniac." I wasn't sure what the word "nymphomaniac" meant, but it sounded intriguing.

"Are you going to prove it tonight?" Steve asked me with a chuckle. Little did I know that he really meant what he had said. Did he realize I had a crush on him?

One day, I walked past his bungalow.

Steve saw me, and said, "Hi, Chris!" There was a

STEVE MCQUEEN AND CHRIS IN "SOLDIER"

Our Sandee Noel Signed For Steve McQueen Movie

By JOHN ROSELLLO
Post-Times Amusements Writer

After a two month long studio search, a blonde, blue-eyed West Palm Beach lass has been dealt the ace of spades in her quest for a successful movie career.

A former "Miss West Palm Beach," five-foot-five Chris Noel — better known locally as Sandee — has been signed by producer Blake Edwards for the romantic role opposite Steve McQueen in "Soldier in the Rain."

Chris was the 11th of the 109 girls tested for the part in the Jackie Gleason—McQueen film and McQueen himself made the test with her just before leaving for location in Monterey, Calif.

Chris, whose name was changed by her New York model agency, is the daughter of Mr. and Mrs. Dave Botz of 2030 Delphia St. and is a graduate of Palm Beach High

SANDEE'S NOW CHRIS

PALM BEACH POST-TIMES JULY 21, 1963

CONFESSIONS OF A PIN-UP GIRL - CHRIS NOEL / 29

warm, inviting tone to his voice.

"Come in!" he said with a broad smile on his face.

Shy but composed, I walked in. Steve was busy working with a heavy-set guy, so I politely excused myself and left. A couple of days later, Steve called me into his bungalow again. This time, no sooner was I in the door than he took me into his arms and began kissing me.

Confused, I broke his embrace and said, "No, No." After all, Steve was married at this time, and unlike so many of the girls in Hollywood, I didn't want to go out with married men.

"But I've been to bed with every one of my leading ladies," Steve insisted.

His piercing blue eyes began to break me down. I felt like I was almost hypnotized by them.

After all, I told myself, this was not just any man, this was Steve McQueen kissing me. He had slept with every one of his leading ladies — who was I to break his perfect record?

I never admitted it before this, but the truth is that we *did* sleep together that night. It was wrong, but to be honest I don't regret it. I mean, *Steve McQueen!*

Several days later, Steve came up and told me, "We've got to talk." He seemed very concerned. Upon getting a positive response from me, his famous blue eyes lit up just like a little kid's — however, this kid was anything but little. He told me that when he was in New York, he lived with two ladies of the evening. For some reason, this revelation made him all the more interesting and exciting to me. And he just wanted to talk to me about his life, especially the painful parts.

Steve had a rare form of cancer called Mesothelioma. I followed news accounts of his trip to Mexico, where he underwent unorthodox treatments in the Plaza Santa Maria Hospital. Members of the press said that even though Steve was wasting away, "you could still see the famous McQueen eyes, piercing, bright blue."

That's exactly how I'll always remember Steve McQueen, the King of Cool.

CONFESSIONS OF A PIN-UP GIRL - CHRIS NOEL / 31

'Soldier in the Rain' Is Warm, Human Film

Rare and choice are the films that can make an audience break up with merriment at one moment and choke up with emotion the next. One such is "Soldier in the Rain," which brings Jackie Gleason, Steve McQueen, and Tuesday Weld to the screen of the Fremont Theater Wednesday.

There's gusto in the Gleason McQueen combination and Tuesday's Bobby Jo Pepperdine is by all odds the most appealing characterization of her career. Then there are Tony Bill, Tom Poston, Ed Nelson, Lew Gallo, and Chris Noel in the other principal roles, and the lyrical musical underscore of the "Moon River" man, Henry Mancini, a star in his own right.

THE CURVACEOUS Miss Noel, whom Hollywood calls "the Method Body," makes a spectacular big-screen debut as McQueen's girlfriend (A-plus). Poston brings chortles as the bedeviled and none-too-bright company commander.

Above Asian and French posters for Soldier In The Rain. The French release was re-titled La Derniere Bagarre, which translates to The Last Brawl.

Left: Movie review -- Miss Noel makes a spectacular big-screen debut as McQueen's girlfriend (A-plus).

Right: Characitures of the cast drawn by noted cartoonist Bruce Stark for the New York Daily News, Nov. 24, 1963.

Soldier in the Rain

Most of the action in the movie, "Soldier in the Rain," occurs in an Army trainee camp, yet principals Jackie Gleason and Steve McQueen find time for a spot of golf. Girl interest is provided by Tuesday Weld (left) and Chris Noel.

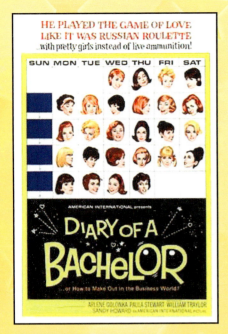

DIARY OF A BACHELOR
Director: Sandy Howard
Studio: American International
Screenplay by: Freddie Francis
Release date: January 1964
Cast: Joe Silver, Dom DeLuise, Paula Stewart, William Traylor, Chris Noel
Length: 89 minutes, black and white
Trivia: Dom DeLuise's first movie, Chris Noel's first film work

Diary of a Bachelor

"DIARY OF A BACHELOR" was a romantic comedy about a wealthy woman who finds her fiancee's diary and reads it, with flashbacks dramatizing the bachelor's sexual exploits day by day, which are actually pretty tame by today's standards. I play one of his old girlfriends, naturally. "Diary" was shot in Manhattan in 1963, in black and white.

The bachelor (William Traylor), is idolized by his poker buddies, romantic washouts who worship his swinging lifestyle. One of his buddies is played by comedian Dom DeLuise, making his movie debut. I knew what Dom felt like, because doing this film was also *my* first time acting in a movie.

Some of my other work was released before this movie, but trust me, my scene in the opening of "Diary" was my first time I had ever acted on film. I didn't say much, and I had to act very excited. It wasn't all that hard, considering how thrilled I was to finally be appearing in a real movie!

DIARY OF A BACHELOR ©1964 AMERICAN INTERNATIONAL

CONFESSIONS OF A PIN-UP GIRL · CHRIS NOEL

HONEYMOON HOTEL
Director: Henry Levin
Studio: Metro Goldywn Mayer
Screenplay by: R.S. Allen and Harvey Bullock
Release date: June 3, 1964
Cast: Robert Goulet, Nancy Kwan, Robert Morse, Jill St. John, Chris Noel
Length: 89 minutes, color
Trivia: Robert Goulet sings the movie's title theme

Honeymoon Hotel

AT THIS TIME, I was under contract with Metro-Goldywn-Mayer. Today, many actors get to pick their own roles, but back then, the studio you were contracted to simply assigned you to roles in the movies they picked out for you.

The second movie they picked for me was a whacky comedy called "Honeymoon Hotel," starring Robert Morse and Robert Goulet.

Goulet was a very handsome man. People used to call him "a walking 8 x 10 glossy." Goulet wasn't horribly vain, but he was well aware of his effect on women, and he seldom passed a mirror without admiring his own reflection.

"Honeymoon Hotel" was one of those fluffy romantic comedies. I only appeared in one scene in this movie — but what a scene! It's set in a singles hotel. Robert Morse is looking for his roommate buddy Robert Goulet. He opens the door to their room, turns on the light, and finds Robert Goulet on the sofa, getting romantic with little old me!

I start to rush out of the apartment, but forget my shoes. Bobby Morse whistles. He's standing by the door, holding them. I take them, then leave as Goulet tells me he'll see me next Tuesday.

It took several takes to get the scene right, but that was fine with me. There are worse things in life than lying on a sofa, kissing Robert Goulet!

ROBERT MORSE, ROBERT GOULET AND CHRIS

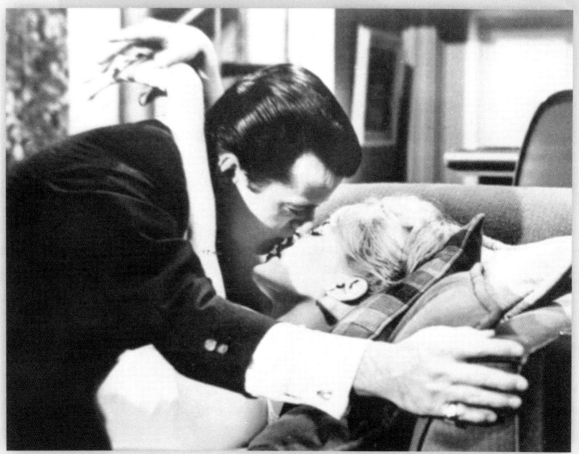

LOOKING FOR LOVE
Director: Don Weis
Studio: Metro Goldywn Mayer
Screenplay by: Ruth Flippen
Release date: November 27, 1964
Cast: Connie Francis, Jim Hutton, Joby Baker, George Hamilton, Johnny Carson, Paula Prentiss, Danny Thomas, Yvette Mimieux, Jesse White, Chris Noel
Length: 84 minutes, color
Trivia: This was the only movie *Tonight Show* host Johnny Carson ever appeared in

Looking For Love

TEEN MOVIES were all the rage, and after "Where The Boys Are" hit it big, MGM tried to cash in by making a series of teenage musicals with similar themes and casts. "Looking For Love," starring Connie Frances and Jim Hutton (who had both appeared in "Boys"), was one of them.

In this movie, I play a stewardess named Flo who plots with Jesse White (TV's Maytag repairman) to get two sets of couples together.

The all-star cast included Danny Thomas, Paula Prentiss, and Yvette Mimieux, who I would later film "Joy In The Morning" with.

Other cast members (see photo on opposite page) included George Hamilton, who I went to High School with in Florida, Joby Baker, who worked with me in "The Glory Stompers," and Johnny Carson, host of *The Tonight Show*, a program I later appeared on several times.

Because of its stellar cast, everyone thought "Looking For Love" would be a huge hit, but unfortunately it didn't turn out that way.

Reviews were definitely mixed. But that didn't bother me at all. Who cared about reviews? This was only my fourth movie, and I was working with some of the top names in film and television!

HATCHING A SCHEME WITH JESSE

Above: Ringing bells with Jesse White, a wonderful man who did hundreds of sitcoms and films, and appeared in TV ads for years as the Maytag Repairman.

Below: This scene from the movie trailer shows George Hamilton, Joby Baker, and former Tonight Show host Johnny Carson.

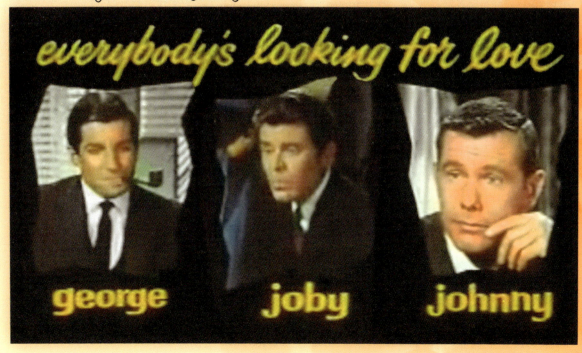

BEWITCHED
Network: ABC
Episode title: "Love Is Blind"
Season: Season 1/Episode 13
Episode number: 13 of 254
Air date: December 10, 1964
Cast: Elizabeth Montgomery, Dick York, Adam West, Chris Noel
Length: 30 minutes, color
Trivia: Chris Noel and Adam West also appear together in "Soldier In The Rain" (United Artists, 1963)

Bewitched

I APPEARED ON lots of different TV shows, but one of my most surprising television experiences came on an early episode of that classic sitcom, *Bewitched*.

In the show, secret witch Samantha tries to set up her spinster girlfriend with Darrin's co-worker, played by Adam West. I had met Adam a year earlier, while doing my first movie, *Soldier In The Rain*.

Darrin tries to ruin Samantha's plan by calling one of Adam's old girlfriends, played by me, and inviting her to dinner. I show up in a good mood, until Samantha uses her witchcraft to make me so angry I walk out of the restaurant!

The surprising part of doing this show was working with Elizabeth Montgomery. That darling-looking woman acted like a *real* witch to me.

She completely ignored me on set, and walked right by me in the hallways. It's not that big a deal, but it was definitely not what I expected out of dear, sweet old Miss Montgomery.

Of course, I wasn't a big star like she was, and neither was Adam West at the time, since this was before he did the smash hit *Batman* TV show.

But still, that was no reason for Montgomery to simply *ignore* her guest cast. I actually got more respect from the talking car on *My Mother The Car!*

CHRIS NOEL AND ADAM WEST

BEWITCHED: "Love Is Blind"

Darrin sets up his friend and co-worker ADAM WEST on a date with Chris, but Samantha isn't happy. She has a spinster girlfriend who she secretly wants West to marry.

Chris and West have dinner with Samantha and Darrin, and everything goes well — TOO well for Samantha. She twitches her nose, works her magic, and causes Chris to undergo an instant personality change.

In a split-second, Chris goes from a happy, engaging dinner companion to the date from hell! She begins arguing ferociously with West, taking issue with everything he says, and insulting him.

West can't understand what's going on, but Samantha is pleased with the outcome: Chris gets up and walks out of the restaurant in a huff, leaving West puzzled and outraged, just as Sam had planned.

The episode ends with Darrin and a happy Samantha attending West's wedding — to Sam's girlfriend, just as she planned all along!

tv notes

ANOTHER MARILYN MONROE?

Blonde Chris Noel is tabbed as successor of late actress

By BOB LARDINE

Chris Noel

Curvy Chris aspires to be another Marilyn Monroe, but she may find that she needs more than a terrific shape and a beautiful face to emulate the fabulous actress

MARILYN MONROE had more than a wiggle and a wicked shape. There were countless other blondes around in her heyday who were just as shapely and beautiful, but Marilyn possessed an innate characteristic which set her apart from them all. No one knows exactly what it was to this day, but no one doubts that she was different.

She could charm intellectuals, though admittedly a "dumb blonde." She could make millions of married men heave heartfelt sighs. And what is really amazing, she could make women envy her without hating her.

Marilyn Monroe was really unique.

When the actress took her own life, a search immediately began in Hollywood to find her replacement. Movie and tv producers were confident it could be done. More than a year has passed since Marilyn's death, and now Metro-Goldwyn-Mayer thinks it has come up with the right gal.

She's 21-year-old Chris Noel, a shapely former model with baby green eyes, and, of course, blonde, silky hair. MGM is so taken with Chris (born Sandra Noel in West Palm Beach, Fla.) that it has signed her to a long term movie pact. She has already been pushed into films, "Diary of a Bachelor" and "Soldier in the Rain." To guarantee maximum exposure, the movie company has also made her a regular on NBC-TV's "The Lieutenant."

Chris is outspoken in her desire to live up to the big build-up. "I'd love to be like her," she says. "But let's face it, what woman wouldn't?"

"Ever since I was a little girl, people have been telling me that I would be 'another Marilyn Monroe.' They even called me Marilyn when I was a kid. Naturally, I've worshipped the actress. I used to cut out pictures of Marilyn when I was younger."

Since she's being mentioned in the same breath with the fabled actress, Chris has begun to compare herself more and more with Marilyn. "Our figures are almost the same. Her measurements were 37-23-34. Mine are 36-23-34. I'm five foot six and Marilyn was an inch taller. My weight stays around 118 while Marilyn was a few pounds heavier."

In her all-out campaign to become a big star, Chris relegates romance and marriage to the background. "I'd never give up my career for a guy," she says emphatically. "I certainly do want to get married some day and have a family, but not right now. I want first to find out how far I can go in the business."

Naturally, Chris is besieged for dates despite the fact that she always makes it clear that wedding bells are not on her mind. "I go out quite a bit, but have no steady boy friend," she says. "I find fellows on the West Coast much nicer than those here in New York. In California they are more considerate, better companions. Men from New York are more selfish, more aggressive, not as gentlemanly. It's actually difficult meeting a nice guy in this city."

Chris, a former Miss Rheingold contestant, lives in a spacious Coldwater Canyon, Calif., house. She shares it with an ex-Miss Rheingold, Kathy Kersh, and an actress-model, Pat Olsen. "We get along just dandy," says Chris. "Personally, I can't see how a girl can live alone. You need someone around who can listen to your troubles. There are plenty of times I feel inadequate, and it's quite nice to have roommates to whom you can confide your disappointments."

When Chris resided in Florida, she entered and won numerous beauty contests. She doesn't think being exceptionally pretty is always a benefit. "I believe most good-looking girls are shy," she says. "In school, I often couldn't get up the courage to stand in front of the class and recite. I've found that unattractive girls have much more nerve. Often, they're downright brazen and have no compunction in telling everyone off."

Chris hated school, and her aversion to books has come to plague her. "My one regret is that I didn't study in school. Now, I'm having to learn how to study, how to discipline myself. I'm terrible at remembering lines," she says.

Of French-Irish ancestry, curvy Chris didn't have too many lines in her previous tv dramatic experience on "The Eleventh Hour." However, few viewers paid much attention to what she said. Most were too busy staring at Chris' figure.

When she isn't training her mind and sharpening her memory, Chris relaxes by swimming and skin-diving. She's proficient at both, but her real talent lies in purring like a feline. Some listeners claim it's one of the sexiest sounds imaginable and Chris has it down to a science. Anyway you look at it, this girl is the cat's meow.

SUNDAY NEWS, OCTOBER 6, 1963

Above Article from the Sunday NY Daily News, October 6, 1963

Opposite page When director John Derek photographed me (in his bedroom), he made me look a lot like two of his wives, Linda Evans and Bo Derek.

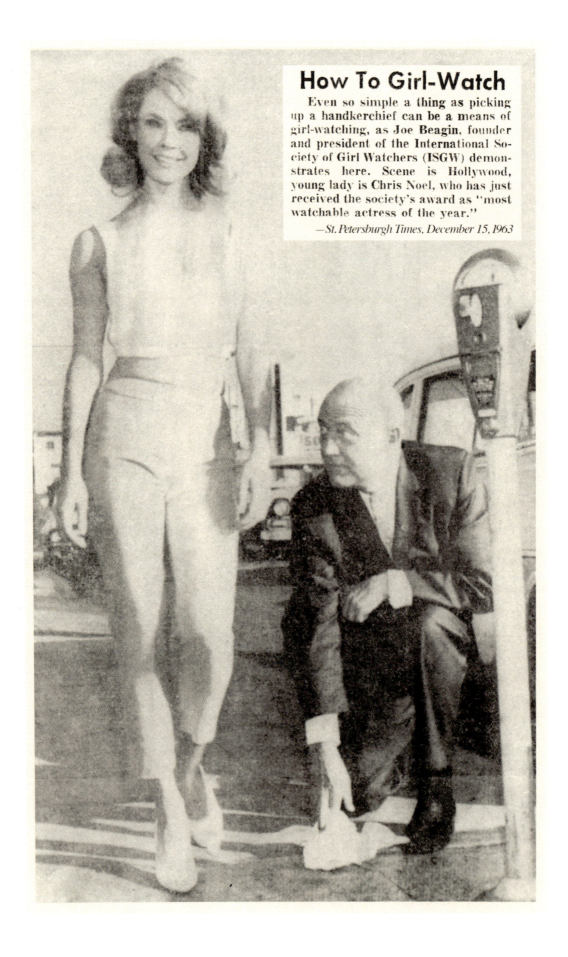

How To Girl-Watch

Even so simple a thing as picking up a handkerchief can be a means of girl-watching, as Joe Beagin, founder and president of the International Society of Girl Watchers (ISGW) demonstrates here. Scene is Hollywood, young lady is Chris Noel, who has just received the society's award as "most watchable actress of the year."

—*St. Petersburgh Times, December 15, 1963*

The New Marilyn Monroe?

Standing awkwardly and lacking makeup and a glamorous hairdo, this slim blonde hardly seems the type to be dubbed "The New Marilyn Monroe." But that's what Hollywood press agents are calling 21-year-old Chris Noel — and maybe that's what Chris is telling this friendly collie at Malibu Beach, Calif.

NATIONAL ENQUIRER - MARCH 8, 1963

ROCKY MOUNTAIN NEWS - SEPTEMBER 20, 1963

Troubles With Bubbles

BLOND CHARMER Chris Noel, to be seen on NBC-TV's The Lieutenant each Saturday night, beginning Sept. 21, says that she was always taught that proper young ladies don't blow bubble gum — but she tried it anyway.

After her bubble trouble Chris decided to stick with the old saying.

"Proper girls should not chew bubble gum — because it's darned near impossible!"

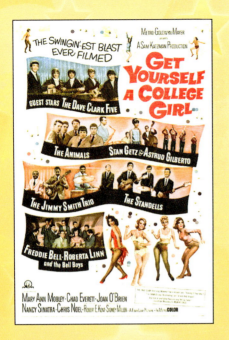

GET YOURSELF A COLLEGE GIRL
Director: Sidney Miller
Studio: Metro Goldywn Mayer
Screenplay by: Robert Kent/Robert Stone
Release date: December 18, 1964
Cast: Mary Ann Mobley, Chad Everett, Fabrizio Mioni, Nancy Sinatra, Chris Noel
Length: 87 minutes, color
Trivia: Originally titled "The Swingin' Set," and released in Europe with that name.

Get Yourself a College Girl aka The Swingin' Set

"COLLEGE GIRL" co-starred Chad Everett (who I dated) and Nancy Sinatra. Nancy and I became friends during filming. It was her second movie, and my fourth. Two years after we did this film, Nancy recorded her smash hit song, "These Boots Were Made for Walkin'." Nancy once told me a touching story about that song.

She said lots of our soldiers in Vietnam had adopted "Boots" as a kind of marching anthem, as seen in the movie "Full Metal Jacket." Hundreds of GI's in Vietnam enjoyed the song so much, they actually mailed her their old combat boots. She got boxes and boxes of them. She got a big kick out of that, and so did I.

We had another connection too -- Elvis! Nancy, standing in for her father, met Elvis at the airport when he returned to America from military service in Germany. Then, a few months later, Nancy and Elvis both appeared on the 1960 television special, "Frank Sinatra's Welcome Home Party for Elvis Presley." Rat packers Joey Bishop and Sammy Davis, Jr., were there too. That amazing show was Nancy's *debut* performance as a professional.

Nancy is a friend, and we've kept in touch since graduating "College." I enjoyed seeing her on HBO's "The Sopranos," playing herself — and I love listening to her weekly program on Sirius Satellite Radio.

P.S. Thanks a million, dear Nancy, for the beautiful introduction you wrote for this book!

FABRIZIO MIONI GETS A GUITAR LESSON

Nancy Sinatra, Chris Noel, Chad Everett, Mary Ann Mobley and Joan O'Brian in scenes from "College Girl," released as "The Swingin Set" in Europe.

THE GO-GO-GO GIRLS . . . Meet the Watusi Dolls. Joan O'Brien, Mary Ann Mobley, Chris Noel and Nancy Sinatra, left to right, cut some fancy watusi steps in MGM's romantic comedy, "Get Yourself a College Girl."

Right: The Iris Movie Theater in West Palm Beach, Florida, 1964, featuring The Dave Clark 5, The Animals, and hometown girl Chris Noel

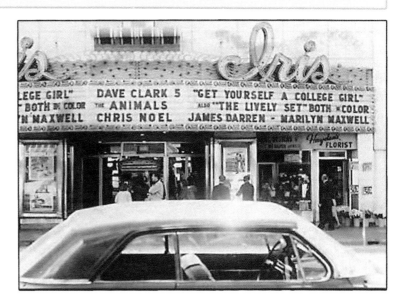

Jack Jones Gives Me a Ring

JACK JONES AND I began dating, and he quickly became my steady boy friend. Jack was a huge singer at this point in his career, with dozens of hit singles to his credit, including "The Impossible Dream," and "Wives and Lovers."

Jack and I went out on the town often, and got written up in the gossip columns regularly. "It's serious," one of them proclaimed, "and he's about to give her a ring!" I thought that was so silly. Jack wasn't about to propose. Or was he? Did they know something I didn't? Was he about to give me a ring? I waited anxiously for him to return from overseas, where he was part of a show Bob Hope was doing in Vietnam.

After the tour ended, Jack returned home, and I was so happy he was back! After many hugs and kisses, he told me, "Honey, I have a big surprise for you!" I gulped. Was this it? The big proposal? Suddenly Jack reached into his jockey shorts (!), and pulled out a ring. Not a diamond, but a beautiful Ruby Princess ring he had bought for me in Thailand. It wasn't a wedding ring.

A few nights later, we threw a wonderful party to celebrate Jack's return. He sang a few songs, then showed slides of his trip with Bob Hope, recounting his experiences entertaining our troops during the Vietnam War — a conflict that would, one day soon, change my entire life.

BURKE'S LAW
Network: ABC

Episode title: "Who Killed Mr. Colby in Ladies' Lingerie?"
Season: Season 2/Episode 24
Episode number: 57 of 65
Air date: March 3, 1965
Cast: Gene Barry, Regis Toomey, Gary Conway, Eileen O'Neill, Chris Noel
Length: 60 minutes, black and white
Trivia: This episode also guest-starred comedian Paul Lynde

Episode title: "Who Killed the Grand Piano?"
Season: Season 2/Episode 31
Episode number: 64 of 65
Air date: April 28, 1965
Cast: Gene Barry, Regis Toomey, Gary Conway, Eileen O'Neill, Chris Noel
Length: 60 minutes, black and white
Trivia: Buke's Law was producer Aaron Spelling's first big hit series

Burke's Law

BURKE'S LAW was a black and white detective series about Amos Burke, the millionaire captain of the Los Angles Police Homicide Division.

Starring as Amos Burke was Gene Barry, who had previously had the title role in TV's "Bat Masterson."

Episodes of "Burke's Law" were basically murder mysteries, and they were always titled "Who killed (name of victim)?" I did two episodes of this series, playing two different characters.

In my first episode, I played Miss Larchmont, a sexy stewardess from "Intimate Airlines" who drives Burke home from the airport because Intimate's motto is: "A stewardess for every passenger, and you're *my* responsibility. Will you fly with us again?"

"With or without plane," Burke deadpans.

I reply, "Well, don't let your wings droop!"

In my second episode of "Burke," I played Patience Stevens, one of many girlfriends the wealthy and handsome Burke had on the show.

When Burke's wild Irish Uncle comes to town for an extended visit, but he winds up spending most of his time with me, making Burke erupt in a fit of jealousy! Until I tell Burke that I'm just *friends* with his uncle, and "with us, it's different."

"Different how?" Burke asks.

I reply by saying "Like this!" and kissing him.

"PATIENCE" AND GENE BARRY

THE HOLLYWOOD REPORTER
FEBRUARY 3, 1965

Chris Noel in 'Lingerie'

Chris Noel has been signed by producer Aaron Spelling to guest in "Who Killed Mr. Colby in Ladies Lingerie," telefilm in the "Burke's Law" series on ABC-TV.

A GIRL NAMED CHRIS NOEL...

turns out to be as much fun as a holiday

Miss Chris Noel, the Sparkle Plenty of the young-actress set and a 1963 Miss Rheingold (Beer) finalist, is an actress born 20 years too late. She really belongs in the heyday of movie hoopla, when she might have had a matched pair of Russian wolfhounds, something "more comfortable" to slip into, and a champagne-filled swimming pool or two to properly set off her talents.

As it happens, Chris is now forced to settle for nonstarring roles in TV and movies and for being (her own description) "the regular roaming, fun-loving girl friend" of Gary Lockwood, both on the screen (in NBC's *The Lieutenant*, in which she is a semiregular) and off it. Nevertheless she manages to bring her own special brand of hoopla into play. She is a good old-fashioned girl who "loves" dressing to the teeth for premieres, silent movies starring John Barrymore, little trips to Catalina (or Las Vegas or San Francisco), night life and swimming pools and men. Moreover, she cries at the movies.

All of which makes Chris a somewhat better show off-screen than on. The daughter of a one-time West Palm Beach police officer, she deliberately set out to storm New York's modeling citadels, got an offer to be a Playboy playmate, and turned it down ("I thought I looked better with my clothes on") in favor of going to Hollywood last June, where she has had "a wonderful time" ever since. She says the reason she set out to be an actress was that as a child she always felt withdrawn. "I hated the feeling," says Chris, whose real name is Sandra Louise Noel. "I liked the recognition a model or an actress gets. A form of exhibitionism, I think."

Chris got a poor start in Hollywood. She signed with Revue, but the management complained she couldn't act and dropped her. Later MGM picked her up in time for the series. Lockwood says, "She's a million laughs." She says Gary is "groovey!" and adds, "I love opinionated men."

She lives in a Coldwater Canyon house with two dogs and three roommates, starts books which she seldom finishes, and applies herself with some—but not too much—diligence to "the No. 2 part of my personality": her talent. As a result she hopes it will catch up with the rest of her. Whatever happens, she expects the "fun, fun, fun" to go on unabated. And at the present moment, no one in Hollywood is betting against it.

10

Above: TV Guide story from the December 21, 1963 issue.

Left: TV Guide story, November 30, 1963.

Below right: A scene from *Burke's Law.*

TV Star Parade, March 1964.

GIRL HAPPY
Director: Boris Sagal
Studio: Metro Goldywn Mayer
Screenplay by: R.S. Allen and Harvey Bullock
Release date: April 7, 1965
Cast: Elvis Presley, Shelly Fabares, Gary Crosby, Nita Talbot, Chris Noel
Length: 96 minutes, color
Trivia: This movie is Elvis' 8th-biggest money-maker, grossing $21,578,624 (inflation-adjusted).

Girl Happy

GIRL HAPPY was set in my native Florida. The movie had Elvis and his band-member buddies secretly chaperoning the daughter of a mobster, played by Shelley Fabares,

Elvis eventually falls in love with Shelly, but then she finds out her father hired him to look after her and wants nothing to do with him. Of course, it all ends happily, when boy gets girl, then performs a rocking rendition of the title song, *Girl Happy*.

I had a relatively small part in this film, but let me tell you, in 1964, it was quite a thrill to play *any* part in a movie starring Elvis Presley!

What was it like working with Elvis? Well, one day on the set, I was sitting on a stool, watching a scene being shot. All of a sudden I felt something wet in my ear. Someone had snuck up behind me and stuck their tongue in my ear.

"Lay off," I exclaimed angrily, then turned around to see who it was.

Yikes! It was Elvis! On seeing him, I turned red. I was so stunned, I didn't know what to do.

"What did you say?" Elvis asked in disbelief. He seemed wounded, as though my angry tone had hurt his feelings. But I didn't know it was him!

What was I supposed to do now, say. "Oh, it's OK, since you're Elvis, you can stick your tongue in BOTH my ears!" I was stuck.

"Well," Elvis finally replied a bit angrily, "If that's how you feel about it — okay."

OFF TO FLORIDA FOR "SPRING FEVER"

"Miss Noel, Elvis wants you right now!"

MY FIRST LINE in "Girl Happy" comes after a phone rings. I pick it up, then tell Shelly Fabares, "Call for you," wearing a blue bathrobe. By the way, under that bath robe, I was totally naked.

After we finished filming the scene, I returned to my dressing room to put some clothes on. But before I could, a member of the film crew started pounding frantically on my door.

I rushed to open it. A man told me, very urgently, "Miss Noel, Mr. Presley wants to take a picture with you right now."

"OK, great!" I replied. "Just let me change."

"There's no time for that Miss Noel," he replied. "Elvis wants you *right now*. Come with me!"

It was a little like being summoned by a President, or a Pope. Or, in this case, a King. Some people are just *not* to be kept waiting! And so, still wearing nothing but my bathrobe, I followed the crew member. He took me to an area nearby that had been set up for a photo shoot.

Elvis was there, along with other female cast members. He grabbed me, told me to stand next to him, and we took the black and white photograph shown on the next page. As you can see, I'm still wearing nothing but that blue bathrobe! But so what — I got my picture with Elvis, and I can never thank him enough for insisting that I take it, bathrobe and all.

Chris Noel and Elvis Presley on the set of Girl Happy.

Screen Life, September 1965

Elvis Serenades Chris... "Leon, Leon" ?!?!

DURING THE FILMING of *Girl Happy,* Elvis had numerous parties, and he invited lots of girls to them — everyone except me. I wondered if he was still mad at me. But then one day, as I was walking down a street on the lot at MGM, Elvis once again snuck up behind me — this time, he started to *sing* to me.

He began singing his own version of the famous Christmas carol, "Noel, Noel," which was fitting because, of course, my last name is Noel. But, for some reason, Elvis decided to change the lyrics. Spelling my last name backwards, he sang to me, "Leon, Leon."

At the time, I thought it was corny, but I was also relieved, because Elvis' antics let me know that things were good between us. Looking back on this small incident, which took all of five minutes and happened a very long time ago, I'm still thrilled to recall that once, Elvis Presley sang just for me.

The blue polka-dot bikini I'm is wearing in these shots didn't come from the MGM wardrobe dept., it came from my own closet!

Opposite page
Relaxing with Shelly on the set.

Left:
Publicity photo.

Below:
Scene from the movie showing Shelly and I on Spring Break in Fort Lauderdale, Florida. The scene was actually shot in California!

CONFESSIONS OF A PIN-UP GIRL · CHRIS NOEL / 65

MGM PRESS KIT
PROGRAM NOTES

Elvis Presley shakes up the campus crowd in his new MGM motion picture, "Girl Happy," in which he delivers a dozen new songs in the hip-hip style that has made him the world's No. 1 record seller.

Elvis, leader of a hot musical combo, has the extracurricular assignment of keeping an eye on lovely Shelley Fabares, who plays the fun-loving daughter of a Chicago night club owner, a perfect role for character actor Harold Stone.

Other young players like Gary Crosby, Bing's son; Mary Ann Mobley, former Miss America; Chris Noel, MGM's current pin-up queen; Joby Baker, fresh from "Honeymoon Hotel," and some 20 bikini-clad lovelies give the film zest and zing.

"Girl" Goes International

GIRL HAPPY was a huge success. It premiered on April 14, 1965, and became one of the top-grossing films of 1965. MGM released it all over the world, creating a different movie poster for almost every country, including England, Spain, France, Italy, Japan, China, Turkey, Sweden and even Yugoslavia.

The publicity photo of me in the polka-dot bikini (shown above) was featured on the Italian and Turkish posters (shown opposite, center and lower right). And get this — a Japanese publication ran a shot of me in that same bikini, and to this day I still have no idea what they said in the article. The same goes for Germany's *Stern (Star)* magazine *(see following pages)*.

CONFESSIONS OF A PIN-UP GIRL-CHRIS NOEL / 67

「雨の中の兵隊」「ハートでキッス」「フロリダ万才」に続いて『カレッジ・ガールにおなりなさい』と、この一、二年で急に映画界に名を広めたクリス・ノエルはテレビのコマーシャル・ガールの出身。いまや青春映画には欠かせぬ存在。

Germany's Stern (Star) magazine.

Elvis rocks and the crowd digs it on these two lobby cards.

"Hello Chris? This is Elvis!"

I STARTED SHOOTING another movie a few weeks after "Girl Happy" wrapped, and most of my scenes were scheduled to be shot *very* early in the morning. I had to get to bed as early as nine, so I could get up and to be on set, ready to go, by 5:00 am.

One night, around 3:00 am, the phone next to my bed rang. I wasn't going to answer it, but it kept ringing and ringing. So I picked it up.

"Hi Chris!" boomed the person on the other end. "How are you? I'm in Europe!"

Still half asleep, I replied, "It's 3:00 in the morning. Who IS this?"

The voice on the other end said, "Elvis!" And it really was him, too. But I was still half asleep, and it didn't really register that THE Elvis Presley was calling me in the middle of the night.

So then — and you probably won't believe this, but it's true — I hung up the phone! I actually hung up on Elvis Presley. *I know, I know...*

The next morning I hardly even remembered what happened, but during the day the phone rang, and that jogged my memory. Suddenly, I remembered that Elvis had called me from Europe, and that I had hung up on him. Worst of all — there was nothing I could do abut it.

This was 1965, long before the invention of such modern conveniences as "redial" or "caller ID." I had no idea how Elvis got my phone number, but I didn't have *his*, and he was still in Europe. I still get upset every time I remember that was the last time I ever spoke to Elvis. But I think of him often, and I'll always be eternally grateful to have had even a small part in a movie starring Elvis Presley, the king of rock 'n' roll.

JOY IN THE MORNING
Director: Alex Segal
Studio: Metro Goldwyn Mayer
Screenplay by: Sally Benson, Alfred Hayes, Norman Lessing
Based on novel by: Betty Smith
Release date: May 5, 1965
Cast: Richard Chamberlain, Yvette Mimieux, Arthur Kennedy, Oscar Homolka, Chris Noel
Length: 103 minutes, color
Trivia: Chris and Richard Chamberlain also appear together in an episode of "Dr. Kildare."

Joy in the Morning

RICHARD CHAMBERLAIN and I had previously done a *Dr. Kildare* episode. In this feature film, Richard plays a college professor, and Yvette Mimieux plays his new bride. The movie is a drama about their stormy marriage.

In one scene, Yvette Mimieux sees me walking around the campus, and being whistled at by some of the boys. She decides to copy my sexy walk. Can you imagine Yvette Mimieux trying to learn how to walk sexy by copying *me?* But that was the scene.

Yvette sort of sneaks up behind me, and follows me as I walk, trying to duplicate my swinging hips. Since the camera is behind us, all you see is our behinds, swinging as we walk along — at first awkwardly, then eventually in unison (see photos on following page).

During shooting, Richard Chamberlain asked me out on a date. At first I was naive enough to think that my big "sexy walk" scene had gotten to him, but during our date I realized pretty quickly that me being romanced by Richard Chamberlain was not going to happen.

One night, Richard took me to a party at Rock Hudson's house. It wasn't my scene, and I wanted to leave early, but Rock insisted that we stay. I don't think Rock cared all that much about *me* — he really just didn't want *Richard* to leave.

FINDING "JOY" – IN A BRUNETTE WIG

DICK AND CHRIS

Dr. Kildare and Miss Noel do some fancy clowning around on the set of "Joy In The Morning." Chris looks great but doesn't the usually handsome Dick look a little like Buster Keaton?

Two really happy, happy people at the height of their careers. Though everyone in Hollywood tried to link them together during this film they're just good friends

Miss Noel and Mr. Chamberlain and the smiles that have won them millions of fans.

CONFESSIONS OF A PIN-UP GIRL - CHRIS NOEL / 73

CHRIS NOEL · CONFESSIONS OF A PSYCHO GIRL

Joy In The Morning

SCENE: The campus of a large, beautiful Ivy League college in the 1920s.

On a warm sunny day, sexy and popular Mary Ellen Kincaid (Chris Noel) rushes to get to class on time.

Shy Annie McGairy Brown (Yvette Mimeau) has been watching Mary Ellen's charms draw the attention of the campus boys like bees to honey. Mary Ellen passes by Annie.

Annie follows Mary Ellen as she walks down a path, heading to class. Annie notices Mary Ellen swinging her hips as she walks and throwing her head back to toss the hair out of her face in an alluring manner.

Me with a brunette wig on!

Annie is quiet and passive. She admires Mary Ellen' bravado, and decides she wants to copy her. She accelerates her pace until she's just a few steps behind Mary Ellen. Both keep walking.

Annie studies Mary Ellen's sexy hip-swinging walk, and begins imitating her. Then she tries to throw her head back in the same pretty, carefree way.

Satisfied with herself, Annie steps up next to Mary Ellen. She begins walking next to her, rather than behind her. The scene ends with the two women walking side by side.

BEACH BALL
Director: Lennie Weinrib
Studio: American International
Screenplay by: Sam Locke
Release date: September 29, 1965
Cast: Edd Byrnes, Chris Noel
Length: 83 minutes, color
Trivia: "Star Wars" producer Gary Kurtz was assistant director of "Beach Ball"

Beach Ball

I STARTED GETTING a reputation as a "beach movie" actress. This wasn't a bad thing back in the days when they cranked out a new teen beach movie almost every week, all year round.

So I signed up to star in *Beach Ball*, a zany comedy about three aspiring rock stars who have to get their instruments out of hock to play a big gig.

To do this, they pose as women, enter a contest, and find themselves competing against such acts as the Righteous Brothers, the Supremes and the Four Seasons. One of the would-be rockers is Edd "Kookie" Byrnes of the TV show *77 Sunset Strip*. I played Edd's love interest in *Beach Ball*. But we didn't get along. At all.

Byrnes thought he was God's gift to women. In real life, he was just like the horn-dog he plays in *Grease*. He had a huge ego, and I had problems working with him. In every kissing scene we did, he kept trying to ram his tongue down my throat!

I eventually got fed up, and warned director Lennie Weinrib that if he didn't make Byrnes stop, I was going to smack him. Lennie spoke to Edd, and his unwanted advances stopped long enough for us to complete the movie, which has since gone on to become a camp cult classic. But I still cringe when I see those awful kissing scenes!

EDD BYRNES GETS AN EYEFUL

Above
Italian poster -- Al Ritmo del Surf (The Rhythm of the Surf).

Right:
A publicity photograph, holding guess what.

Above
Having a ball on the beach.

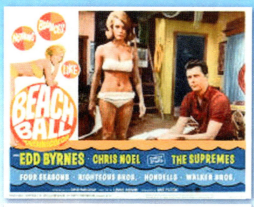

Lobby cards featuring the cast, including Chris, Edd, plus Diana Ross and the Supremes, third row down, on the right.

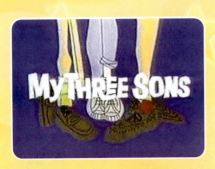

MY THREE SONS
Network: CBS
Episode title: "Marriage and Stuff"
Season: Season 6/Episode 13
Episode number: 197 of 380
Air date: December 10, 1965
Cast: Fred MacMurray, William Demarest, Stanley Livingston, Don West, Chris Noel
Length: 30 minutes, color
Trivia: The face of comic book superhero Captain Marvel (Shazam!) was modeled after Fred MacMurray

My Three Sons

MY THREE SONS was a sitcom about widower Steven Douglas (Fred MacMurray) raising his three sons with the help of his housekeeper, Uncle Charlie.

The show was hugely popular, producing a record 380 episodes, more than any other show except "Ozzie and Harriet."

Most sitcoms in this era filmed their scenes "in sequence," which means scenes were shot in the same order in which they'd appear. "My Three Sons" did thing differently. At Fred's insistence.

Each year, Fred MacMurray would shoot all his scenes for the entire season in about two months — and not in order. For example, all the living room scenes would be done together, then all the kitchen scenes, and so on. Guest stars did their scenes with Fred during this time, then returned months later to do their scenes with members of the supporting cast, and complete their episode.

Following this practice, I did my scenes with Fred, then returned a few weeks later to do another scene with Robby (Don Grady, pictured right).

In my episode, a mix-up leads the Douglas family to believe that their father and I are getting married. At the time, I was in my twenties and Fred was 57, but never mind that. It's a sitcom!

FRED MacMURRAY AND HIS "FIANCE"

Burt Reynolds: A Truly Sensuous Man

ON A TRIP back home to Florida, I was introduced to Burt Reynolds. Burt was gregarious among crowds — but when he was alone with me, he was frequently moody and quiet. He wanted to be a star in the worst way. One day he would be a top box-office draw, but it hadn't happened yet.

Nevertheless, he was a handsome, tremendously sexy man, and when he invited me to stay in his New York apartment, I accepted. Burt's bedroom was dark, with a king-sized bed and satin sheets that kept slipping off onto the floor. Burt is truly a sensuous man.

A lot of Burt's friends called him Buddy, and I, too, came to call him by that nickname. We dated several times, in New York, Florida and California. Dating Burt was wonderful, but one thing about it was particularly aggravating — he was *never* on time!

Our last date was on February 11th — Burt's birthday. I had fixed an intimate dinner for him. He arrived late, as usual. Because he loved boating, I had bought him what I thought was a perfect gift: a scale-model yacht. But when he opened it, it didn't seem to thrill him much. We went on with our meal, and he became quiet. Apparently, he had been expecting a big party with all his friends rather than an intimate dinner. After we finished the meal, he thanked me and abruptly left.

We never dated again, but we made up years later, when he cast me in a TV-movie featuring his B.L. Stryker detective character. Burt once told me that I was the only girl he ever dated who never asked him for anything.

WILD WILD WINTER
Director: Lennie Weinrib
Studio: Universal Studios
Screenplay by: David Malcolm
Release date: January 5, 1966
Cast: Gary Clarke, Chris Noel
Length: 80 minutes, color
Trivia: This movie, director Lennie Weinrib's second after "Beach Ball," was originally titled "Snow Ball."

Wild Wild Winter

HAVE YOU EVER HEARD of a beach movie that takes place at a ski resort? Well, that was the idea behind "Wild Wild Winter."

I played a ski instructor who is being chased by Gary Clarke. There was only one small problem — I had never been skiing in my entire life, and had absolutely no idea how to do it! And here I was playing a ski instructor. How did that happen?

Well, when they offered me this part, they asked me, "Can you ski?" When you're an actress and you want a part, whenever they ask if you have some particular skill or talent, you just automatically say yes. So I told them, "Sure, I can ski!"

Then they said, "Oh, that's good, because you're going to be playing a ski *instructor*."

Gulp! "Oh well," I thought, "I'll fake it somehow. What could happen?"

If you look closely at the movie, you'll see that in my skiing scenes, I can barley stand up. I'm supposed to be teaching Gary to ski, but in reality he's actually holding ME up, and making me look good. But even with Gary's help, you can still see me slipping and sliding all over the place, as I pretend to be an "expert." At least I managed to finish filming without breaking a leg.

And to this day, I have *never* been skiing!

WILD WILD WINTER LOBBY CARD

My Date With Frank Sinatra

FRANK PICKED ME UP at my house in LA. for what I thought was going to be an intimate dinner, just the two of us. But as we drove down Sunset Strip, I noticed a car was following closely behind us. I asked Frank about it.

Shrugging his shoulders, he said, "Those are my friends."

We went to an Italian place on the Sunset Strip. At the restaurant, the maitre d' took us to a large table with several place settings. I was about to ask Frank why the table was so big, when suddenly several men came over and joined us. I was disappointed that Frank and I were not going to dine alone, but I realized that this was just part of Frank's way of doing things, so I went along with it.

All during dinner, Frank's friends kept on talking about a certain actress — Mia Farrow. They went on and on about how Mia was so different from other women they knew. Frank hardly said a word during the entire meal, and I did likewise.

After dinner, we all went to a nightclub for a drink. After about twenty minutes, at Frank's signal, we all got up and went to another nightclub, for another drink. After about an hour, Frank once again signaled it was time to leave. Outside this particular club, a man stepped out of the darkness and began whispering to Frank. After what seemed like a heated discussion, Frank ordered one of his friends to give the man what looked like a large amount of money. We got in the car and drove to Frank's place.

At Sinatra's house, we sat around having yet another drink. For some reason, Frank got up and began to pace back and forth. He walked over to a sliding glass door, and all of a sudden he began to kick it. Then, to everyone's amazement, he shattered the glass with a single punch! We sat there, stunned. No one said a word. It was absolutely incredible.

After about ten minutes, Frank suddenly came and sat next to me on the couch. He kissed me gently on the mouth, then whispered to me, "I'm taking you home."

The ride was brief and silent. At my house, Sinatra took my keys, unlocked the door, kissed me again, and said, "See you around, kid."

What a memorable date — I couldn't have asked for better entertainment! But it was obvious to me that Sinatra had another woman on his mind the entire evening. And, sure enough, shortly afterwards, on July 19, 1966, Frank Sinatra married the young girl who was "so different from other women he knew" — Mia Farrow.

To everyones amazement, Frank shattered the glass door with a single punch! We sat there, stunned. No one said a word. It was absolutely incredible.

FRANK SINATRA IN PAL JOEY © COLUMBIA PICTURES INDUSTRIES, INC./OPPOSITE PAGE: PHOTO BY RALPH KEENAN

CONFESSIONS OF A PIN-UP GIRL-CHRIS NOEL / 87

HOLLYWOOD PALACE
Network: ABC
Season: Season 4/Episode 22
Episode number: 114 of 192
Air date: February 25, 1967
Host: Van Johnson
Length: 60 minutes, black and white
Trivia: This episode featured the American debut of the Beatles' music videos for "Penny Lane" and "Strawberry Fields Forever"

Hollywood Palace

THE HOLLYWOOD PALACE was a variety show that ran from Jan. 4, 1964 to Feb. 7, 1970.

Each show usually featured an all-star cast, so I was thrilled to appear on it, along with George Carlin, Liza Minnelli and *The Beatles!!*

When they told me The Beatles were going to be on the show, I couldn't believe my luck. I was so excited to be meeting them in person — but it didn't turn out that way.

Unfortunately, the Fab Four weren't *there* in person. They were just appearing in music videos of "Penny Lane" and "Strawberry Fields Forever."

Oh well! There went my big dreams of kissing Paul McCartney and hugging John Lennon. But I did get to hear Liza sing "Cabaret."

"The Hollywood Palace" didn't have just one host. A different celebrity took over hosting duties each show, or sometimes the same celeb would host several shows in a row.

When I was on, the host was Van Johnson (pictured below), a talented singer, dancer and matinee idol who had starred in dozens of movies, including "Divorce, American Style."

I was deeply honored to have appeared on "Palace," because I felt it meant I had truly made it in the business. Me, on the same show with George Carlin, Liza, and The Beatles!

I'll never forget my night at the Palace.

VAN JOHNSON AND CHRIS

 GEORGE CARLIN
 LIZA MINNELLI
 THE BEATLES

BEATLES PHOTO © APPLE CORPS.

VACATION PLAYHOUSE
Network: CBS
Episode title: "The Good Old Days"
Season: Season 4/Episode 1
Air date: July 11, 1966
Length: 30 minutes, black and white
Trivia: One of the few shows Chris appeared in that was not set in contemporary times.

Vacation Playhouse

IN THE GOOD OLD DAYS, producers used to present their ideas for new television series to the networks by shooting a "pilot" episode, which gave people a rough idea of what a potential series would be like.

Sometimes the series was picked up, but more often it was not, and the pilot was left to gather dust in a storeroom, doomed to remain unaired.

That's what almost happened to a pilot I did called "The Good Old Days." It was a whacky satire, a sitcom set way back in prehistoric days.

I played "Pantha," and Darryl Hickman (pictured opposite, dragging me up a stone-age ladder) was a caveman named "Rok."

CBS was not impressed by the pilot, and declined to buy the show as a regular series. But instead of leaving it unaired, CBS decided to run the pilot we shot as part of their anthology series "Vacation Playhouse."

Unfortunately, "Good Old Days" didn't set any ratings records, so the show was quickly forgotten, and it was never aired again.

So much for my career as a cavewoman!

ROK AND PANTHA HAVE A TALK

Tonight's Best Bets

Vacation Playhouse: "The Good Old Days." An unsold comedy pilot starring Darryl Hickman and featuring Chris Noel. The plot: A teen-age caveman leaves his family and finds living alone less exciting than he anticipated.

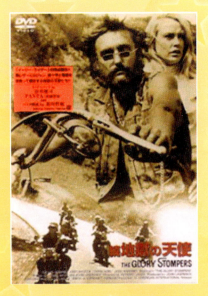

THE GLORY STOMPERS
Director: Anthony M. Lanza
Studio: American International
Screenplay by: James Gordon White and John Lawrence
Release date: January 1968
Cast: Dennis Hopper, Chris Noel
Length: 85 minutes, color
Trivia: Chris and Dennis Hopper also appeared together in "Wild Times," a TV mini-series set in the old west.

The Glory Stompers

I WENT FROM beach balls to bad boy bikers in "The Glory Stompers," a wild movie starring the late Dennis Hopper.

In previous films, I had romped across the beaches of America without a care, having fun. But in this movie, I get kidnapped by the leader of a motorcycle gang (Dennis Hopper). The gang abuses me in every possible way: I get beaten, chased through the woods, tied up, and sexually assaulted. Quite a change from lounging around the beaches of California with Elvis!

Dennis Hopper appeared in more than 140 TV shows, but he's probably most famous for his roles in the films "Easy Rider" (1969), "Apocalypse Now" (1979), and "Speed" (1994).

Dennis was an accomplished photographer. One day near the end of shooting for this movie, he stood up and declared, "This movie stinks! I'm a director, and I can make it better."

With that, Dennis proceeded to take control of the days' shoot, directing several shots of rowdy bikers silhouetted against the desert sunset. Dennis never got any official credit for his work, which only took up a minute of screen time. But still — everyone had to admit that the scenes he shot were really spectacular. Call him crazy, but Dennis directed what turned out to be the best-looking scenes in the entire movie.

CHRIS KIDNAPPED BY DENNIS HOPPER

The abuse I take during this movie is scary.

Above
Dennis took this candid shot of me relaxing between takes.

Right:
A boy, a girl, a bike.

Opposite page
As I was taking this candid shot of Dennis, he stuck a prop gun into his pants! He was a real wild man.

Above
Dennis Hopper and his kidnap victim.

Left: Biker chick goes on the attack.

Dig this Asian Stompers poster. Oh my!

FOR SINGLES ONLY
Director: Arthur Dreifuss
Studio: Columbia Pictures
Screenplay by: Hal Collins and Arthur Dreifuss
Release date: June 5, 1968
Cast: Milton Berle, John Saxon, Mary Ann Mobley, Lana Wood, Chris Noel
Length: 91 minutes, color
Trivia: The first and only film to show Chris Noel semi-naked

For Singles Only

MY BITCHIEST ROLE, without a doubt, was a character named Lily who lived in a swinging apartment complex "For Singles Only."

Lily was like a forerunner to Joan Collins in "Dynasty." She smoked, she drank, she was always plotting against rivals, and she had a wicked tongue. The picture on the opposite page shows Lily competing in a wild psychedelic body-painting contest.

I enjoyed playing Lily quite a bit, except for one scene where I was supposed to take off my swim-top, partially exposing one of my breasts. Even though it was more suggestive than explicit, I was still nervous about the whole thing.

We filmed my "nude" scene on a closed set, with me wearing pasties over my real breasts. The director, Arthur Dreifuss, even had my character's boyfriend (Peter Richman) stand in front of me. His shirt sleeve was strategically positioned to block the audience's view (see photo below), just like they did in "Austin Powers." Groovy, baby!

Compared to all the totally explicit stuff in movies today, this scene seems almost PG-rated. But still, it was the closest I ever came to appearing nude on the big screen.

SEMI–NAKED WITH PETER RICHMAN

The Pop Artist and the Swami

SWAMI SATCHIDANANDA was a spiritual master who lived in India, but moved to America after a visit with his pupil, famous pop artist Peter Max. Satchidananda was the opening speaker at the Woodstock music festival.

I once attended one of Swami Satchidananda's ashrams. Quite an amazing experience. It was just myself and a small group of people at a secluded commune in upstate New York.

For ten days, we got up at sunrise, and went to bed at sunset. It was a silent retreat, so there was no talking, plus everyone had to dress all in white. I loved my white outfit!

One morning, we hiked to a small stream. Each of us had to drink gallon of water from it, then throw up back into it. This was supposed to cleanse us of impurities. After that, we returned to the compound, where we were baptized with a shower of rose petals. I can still remember their wonderful fragrance.

Over the next ten days we did similar things, and also listened to speeches by some of Swami Satchidananda's followers, including artist Peter Max, creator of dazzlingly colorful pop-art paintings that perfectly captured the spirit of the Sixties — just like my fascinating experiences at the Swami's retreat.

Above
Peter Max with his guru, Swami Satchidananda.

Below:
The Yantra, a geometric design used by Eastern mystics to focus the mind on spiritual concepts.

Warren said with a kind of begrudging admiration, "Wow. You're like a female version of me!"

"Hello Chris? This is Warren Beatty."

ONE DAY, I got another one of those phone calls I'll never forget. I was home in bed with the flu at the time.

It began: "Hello Chris? This is Warren Beatty."

"Uh, hi Warren," I answered, "What do you want?"

"I'm visiting friends next door," Warren said. "Could I come over and borrow a cup of sugar?"

"Sorry, we don't use sugar," I told him, "And I'm sick in bed right now."

But Warren wasn't giving up that easily. He called back twice, asking if he could come over. I told him no repeatedly, explaining that I had the flu. Then the phone rang *again*. This time, it wasn't Warren — it was his sister, Shirley McLaine (their mother's surname was McLaine, and their father's was Beaty. Warren's real full name was Henry Warren Beaty — he added an extra "t" to his last name, I guess to make it easier to pronounce).

Apparently Shirley was with Warren at the time, next door to me. She was apparently mad that I had given her brother the brush off. She called to say just one word to me.

"Bitch!" Shirley McLaine exclaimed. And with that said, she hung up the phone.

True story, so help me. And there's more. A lot more.

I had read countless articles in gossip magazines about Warren's sexual exploits. I didn't want to get seriously involved with him, but I curious to find out if all the stories were true.

Two years later, I did. Warren called me again, and this time I invited him over. We wound up spending the night together, at my house in LA. What a night!

Warren wasn't a world-famous actor/director yet, but he did have an amazing reputation for being a great lover. And as I found out, that reputation was very well-deserved. We had a wild night of romance that lasted until sunrise.

Around noon, I finally got up, took a shower, and began straightening up my house. Warren was still there, but I pretty much ignored him. Our night together was over, and I wasn't interested in anything more.

"Wow," Warren said with a kind of begrudging admiration, "You're like a female version of ME!"

"So how does it feel?" I asked him.

Warren just sat there and stared at me. No reply!

PHOTO: LOUIS GALANOS

PART THREE
Goodbye Hollywood, Hello Vietnam

ON CHRISTMAS DAY 1965, a goup of celebrities went to Balboa and Letterman Veterans Administration hospitals in San Diego and San Francisco, to visit soliders wounded in the Vietnam War.

The group included California Governor Brown, comedians Dan Rowan and Dick Martin, baseball legend Sandy Koufax, Milton Berle's wife Ruth, as well as roommate, Eileen O'Neill, and myself.

Visiting the hospital that day changed my life. I was a young girl, with many wonderful things in my life, but at the hospital that day, I realized how naive I had been. While I had been partying in Hollywood, here in this hospital and others like it, hundreds of brave, wounded soldiers were struggling to just to *survive*. It changed me forever.

Surprisingly, most of the GI's were smiling as we entered the gangrene ward — full of double and triple amputees. They were trying to survive by laughing, by grabbing a few minutes of fun. At that moment, I realized the importance of a friendly smile to these men.

The whole scene upset me, but I held my tears back. Years of acting had taught me how to smile when I didn't feel like it. I decided then and there that I was going to dedicate myself to supporting our troops in Vietnam, and all around the world.

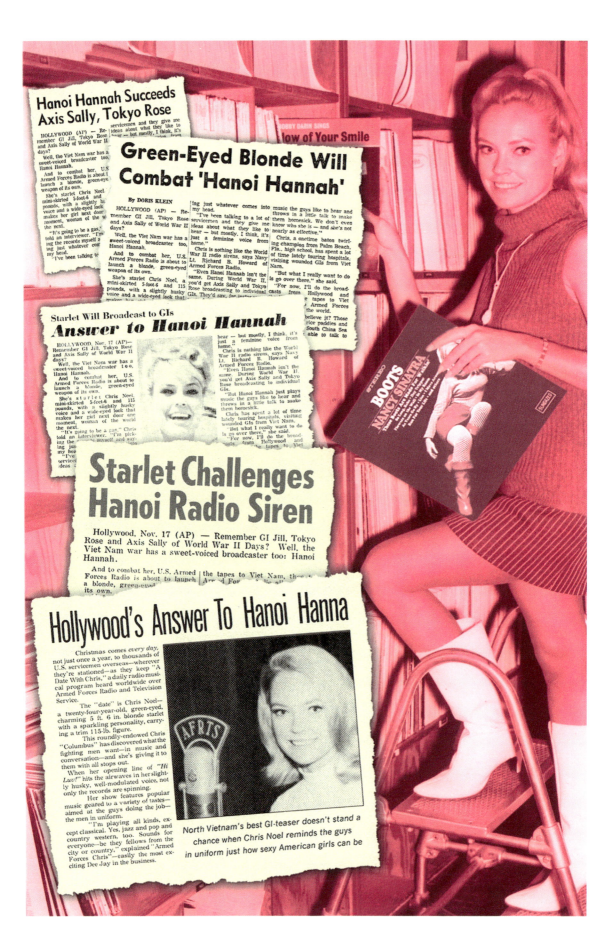

Hollywood's Answer to Hanoi Hannah

THE VIET CONG had a propaganda radio host known as *Hanoi Hannah*. She was like a Vietnam version of WWII's "Tokyo Rose," trying to demoralize our soldiers in Vietnam. The Pentagon hired me to give our troops someone to listen to besides Hanoi Hanna.

In 1966, I became a DJ for Armed Forces Radio, broadcasting a daily hour-long radio show heard worldwide by our fighting forces. I was the first woman since World War II to have such a show. I began each of my programs, called *A Date With Chris*, by saying "Hi love!"

My show was such a success in building morale that even the enemy recognized me. The Vietcong actually put a price on my head — of $10,000. I was flattered, but not scared a bit. How could I be? I was constantly surrounded by soldiers!

My program became a huge hit, and my pin-ups began appearing in our military installations all over the world, especially in Vietnam. Forget about movies, I was a pin-up girl — and *proud of it!*

I became a DJ for Armed Forces Radio and Television Station in 1966.

Ray Ambrozy, Charlie Company 3/60 9th Div. with company mascot Buddy, and the pin-up seen opposite.

PHOTO © RAY AMBROZY

Cartoons by Corky Trinidad (top, bottom), and Jim Judd (center).

A DATE WITH CHRIS - TRANSCRIPT

Hers a summarized transcript of one of my shows. Besides playing the latest songs, I read mail from our troops around the world, made songs dedications, and read public service announcements.

HI LOVE! Welcome everybody, to another Date with Chris! I'm Chris Noel, with all kinds of good sounds for you. This program is brought to you by Armed Forces Radio.

Billy of Battery 6/15 Artillery writes: "I have a question for you, Chris. How short are the dresses in the states now? The shorter the better!"

Well I have good news for you, Billy. They're still short. The mini-skirt is still in. The hemline is about 12 inches above the kneecap. That's right. All the girls are running around in our mini-skirts. Billy also asked that I play a song for a groovy group of guys — Ernie, Chucky Poo, Harvey, Tom Tom, Skee Man, Tomato — sounds like a wild group. To open my program, here's a Dionne Warwick song for you guys, high on the charts, "This Girl's In Love With You."

Let's open to the mailbag! I received a nice letter from Stephen Brown aboard the USS Redford. It seems Stephen has a problem."Everyone knows how crowded it is on a destroyer, but we have a blank space on one bulkhead. It's just a shade over a foot square, right next to a receiver we use to tune to your show." Steve wants me to send him a picture to hang up in that space. It's on the way, autographed to you, Steve, and to all the guys on the USS Redford. And here's a tune by the Beatles, called "Come Together."

Now, back to our program. I have a letter from PFC Vell with Headquarters Batt. 3rd Batt. 11th Marines, 1st Marine Division. He thanks me for the good music, and asks me to play a song for all his buddies. Here it is, "The Letter" by the Box Tops.

A soldier in the 7th Communications Batt., Battalion Supply stationed in Danang asks me to play a song for his buddy from his hometown, Kane Penn. He tells me his Buddy is out in the bush, and he's in Danang. The Buddy is fellow Marine Rod Ficus, K company, 3rd of the 7th, 60th Mortars of the 1st Marine Div. He wants to dedicate it to his friend, who is working hard in the bush. Anyway fellas, the song is for both of you, Here's one of the real groovy tunes of the day, "Downtown" by Petula Clark.

This is Chris Noel, playing the songs you requested, songs from the Top 40 list in the States, songs your girlfriends, wives and families are listening to, day after day.

A lot of mail comes from you "Screaming Eagles." Other guys write as a group, too. Today, I heard from the 5th Transportation Company. PFC Milton from Raleigh, N.C, Sp4 Jim from Orlando, Florida, Sp4 Bob from California, and Sp4 Gene of Mansfield, Ohio. They say they never miss one of my shows! Thanks fellas.

Here's a song for y'all... oops, my Southern accent is coming out... now we'll spin one by a leading lady on the charts, Diana Ross and the Supremes, singing their big hit, "Stop, In The Name Of Love!"

I love to receive your letters, and I read all the letters you send me. Most of you request pictures of me in a mini-skirt... they're on the way! If you have requested a picture, it should be reaching you in the next few weeks. And I'm not forgetting our troops stationed in Korea, Europe and all over rest of the free world.

Guys, I've put you all down in my date book for another musical meeting tomorrow at the same time. Don't stand me up, okay? Here's "Miss Christmas," signing off with a kiss from Chris ... **BYE LOVE!**

This is the United States Armed Forces Radio And Television Service.

> When Chris opens with *"Hi Luv!"* in her husky, low-register voice, GI ears stand "at attention" while the rest of their bodies are "at ease." For an hour they relax to their favorite musical numbers and the *sexy voice in the night*—the "image of the girl back home."
> Then Chris signs-off with the now-familiar: "Bye Luv!" and a resounding kiss crackles the airwaves. A collective sigh arises from military barracks all over the world. Uncle Sam's warriors just had a DATE WITH CHRIS.
>
> **STARS AND STRIPES, DECEMBER 1966**

S/4 John Schultz in Duc Pho, Vietnam, with his favorite pin-up.

Thomas Magnum in Vietnam, listening to the mysterious Holly Fox on the radio.

Magnum's "Case of the Disguised DJ"

MAGNUM, P.I. starring Tom Selleck, often had plots that revolved around the Vietnam War, because Thomas Magnum, as well as his friends Rick and T.C., were all supposed to be Vietnam veterans. Magnum's pal Higgins, by the by, was too old for duty in Nam.

The *Magnum* episode "The Look" (Season 4, Episode 9, first aired December 8, 1983), featured a fictionalized version of me named Holly Fox (played by Gretchen Corbett). Holly was a blonde disc jockey who Magnum and his friends had idolized as soldiers during the Vietnam War.

Above Magnum's fictionalized version of me.

How do I know this character was based on me? Well, to begin with, I was the only female at this time with a radio show heard by our soldiers in Vietnam. In a flashback scene, Holly reads dedications to our troops in Vietnam, just like I did. And it can't be a coincidence that "Noel" and" "Holly" are both Christmas names. She also wears her blonde hair a lot like I did when this episode was filmed, and she is menaced, on a beach (!) by a wild biker right out of "Glory Stompers." Don't worry, though, Magnum saves her.

Watching this show was a little like seeing a weird dramatization of my life where they somehow got my name wrong! Oh well. Anything to get close to gorgeous Tom Selleck — even if it was only a fictionalized version of myself.

CHRIS NOEL VISIT TO VIETNAM - Chris prepares to debark a 1st Air Cavalry Division helicopter at An Khe, 21 December 1966. Photo by Captain Willis J. Haas, Jr., USA.

Sex Kitten Arrives to Combat Reds

Chris Noel is Hollywood's answer to Hannoi Hannah, the latter-day Tokyo Rose who spouts radio propaganda to our troops in Vietnam. "They were interviewing girls for the purpose of putting one on the air," recalls Noel. "So I made an appointment for an interview, and answered their questions and did a kind of mock radio show...

Christmas in Vietnam

SOON AFTER my radio program clicked, the Pentagon began making plans for me to go Vietnam in person. In preparation, I went to the 6592nd USAF Dispensary (AFSC) in Los Angeles and got vaccinations for Smallpox, Cholera, Tetanus, Plague, Flu, Yellow Fever and Typhoid! Ouch, my aching arm.

The Department of Defense takes no chances, especially with civilians going overseas. I took my shots all at one time. What a mistake that was. I got so sick I almost couldn't go! But with some help from a few soldiers, I dragged myself onto a plane, and off I went — for the first of what many trips to various locations all over Vietnam. I was only allowed to take ONE suitcase per trip. I used the same one every time, bright red leather.

When my plane arrived in Vietnam at Tan Son Nhut, I didn't expect anyone to recognize me, and they didn't — at first. But a few minutes after I landed, a jeep full of soldiers suddenly drove up, and one of them began yelling, "Outstanding! Number One! That must be her! That's Chris Noel!" Then slowly, a crowd began to form around me. I smiled and waved, my heart pounding.

I thought, "Goodbye Hollywood, hello Vietnam!"

CONFESSIONS OF A PIN-UP GIRL by CHRIS NOEL/123

Chris and Ron Disney, aka Diz, at Camp Evans May 1968.

GETS HARD LOOK — A native Saigon woman in traditional costume looks sharply at the mini-skirt sported by Chris Noel, 26, disc jockey from West Palm Beach, who has joined the Armed Forces Radio in Vietnam to counter Hanoi Hannah, who nightly purrs anti-Americanism and news between music for U.S. troops.

The Tank Incident

WEARING MY MINI-SKIRT in the streets of Saigon caused an uproar, but that was nothing compared to almost making a tank drive off the road. Reporter Hugh Mulligan put it this way, in the Associated Press article shown on the next page:

"The tank driver could be pardoned for wandering off the road and almost mowing down a row of rubber trees. It isn't every day a soldier sees a green-eyed blonde in thigh-high miniskirt and saucy white boots tramping around the perimeter while the howitzers bang away and helicopters roar off to war. But then, every Infantry doesn't have an adopted daughter like Chris Noel. Only the Big Red One — the U.S. First Infantry Division — can proudly make that claim, even if it may cost them a tank or truck or two running amok here and there."

Below:
1st Infantry Division (Big Red One) patch.

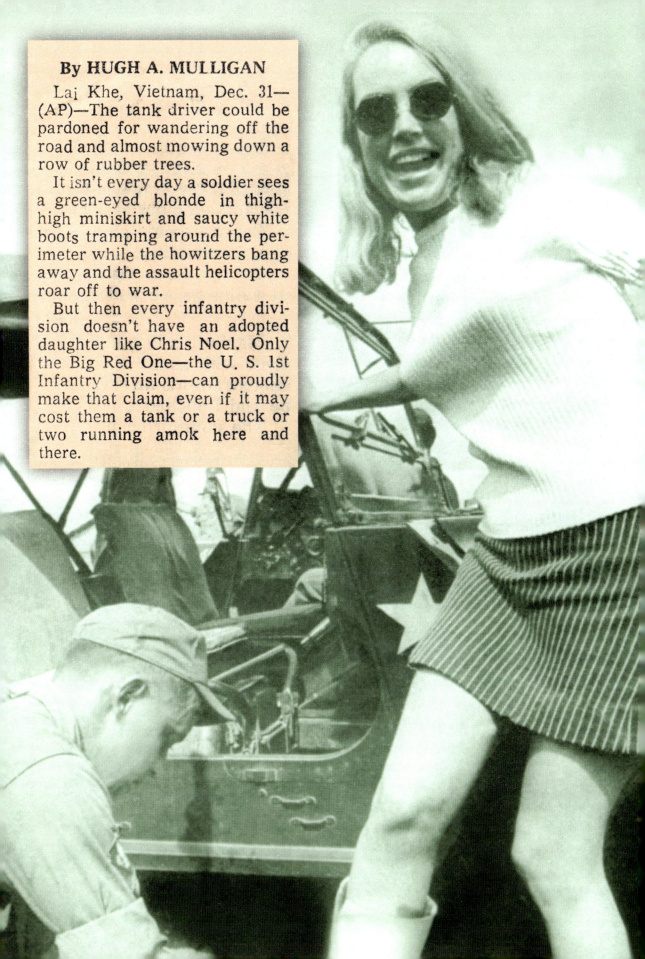

By HUGH A. MULLIGAN

Lai Khe, Vietnam, Dec. 31—(AP)—The tank driver could be pardoned for wandering off the road and almost mowing down a row of rubber trees.

It isn't every day a soldier sees a green-eyed blonde in thigh-high miniskirt and saucy white boots tramping around the perimeter while the howitzers bang away and the assault helicopters roar off to war.

But then every infantry division doesn't have an adopted daughter like Chris Noel. Only the Big Red One—the U. S. 1st Infantry Division—can proudly make that claim, even if it may cost them a tank or a truck or two running amok here and there.

Performing on the deck of the U.S.S. Ticonderoga, in the Gulf of Tonkin, Vietnam

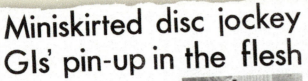

Miniskirted disc jockey GIs' pin-up in the flesh

She's a 5-foot-6, 115 pound package of dynamite with the platters and patter that really sends 'em

LET'S FACE IT. Jumping up and down and yelling Sis-Boom-Bah isn't show biz.

But for a girl with the rather unostentatious name of Sandra Louise Botz, it was a beginning. The audience was big at those New York Giants football games, but she was leading the cheers instead of receiving them. And, the pay wasn't much: $10 for an afternoon of yelling her head off.

Then during one long, hot summer, Sandra Botz, who was already near the mid-twenties point, was born again. To say she was "rechristened" would sound

STARS AND STRIPES

CHRIS NOEL'S LOVE AFFAIR WITH HALF-A-MILLION MEN

Pretty, blonde Chris Noel—dressed in a set of GI fatigues—leaned against a jeep and laughed.

"Me, a propagandist!" she said in response to our question of whether she considered herself one. "Don't be ridiculous.

"I'm just a girl who's trying to make the men she loves happy. You see, I'm in love with half-a-million guys—all the American troops in Vietnam."

NATIONAL ENQUIRER

H.H.C., 11th Infantry Brigade, Duc Pho, Vietnam, May 1968

Touring Chris Noel Rings The Bell With Our Boys Up Front

LAI KHE, Vietnam — (AP) — The tank driver could be pardoned for wandering off the road and almost mowing down a row of rubber trees.

It isn't everyday a soldier sees a green-eyed blonde in thigh high miniskirt and saucy white boots tramping around the perimeter while the howitzers bang away and the assault helicopters roar off to war.

But then every infantry division doesn't have an adopted daughter like Chris Noel. Only the Big Red One—the U.S. ... little portable phonograph that she carries everywhere.

She pulled the lanyard on a 105 howitzer, after first signing the shell "to Charlie, lots of luck, Chris," and nearly jumped out of her courages boots when the round went ripping off into an abandoned rubber plantation five miles away.

She dropped in on an orientation lecture for newly arrived replacements and left the orientation officer to resume his talk with a stammered "men, as I was saying about booby traps . . ."

MIAMI NEWS

OUR NEWEST WEAPON IN VIETNAM

POLICE GAZETTE

Chris Is Big Thrill For GIs in Vietnam

By HUGH A. MULLIGAN

LAI KHE, Vietnam (AP)—The tank driver could be pardoned for wandering off the road and almost mowing down a row of rubber trees.

It isn't everyday a soldier sees a green-eyed blonde in thigh high miniskirt and saucy white boots tramping around the perimeter while the howitzers bang away and the assault helicopters roar off to war.

But then every infantry division doesn't have an adopted daughter like Chris Noel. Only the Big Red One—the U.S. 1st Infantry Division—can proudly make that claim, even if it may cost them a tank or a truck or two rubber trees here and there.

The sultry voiced disc jockey who is armed forces radio's all out answer to Hanoi Hannah was officially adopted by the 15,000-man division when she was in Vietnam over Christmas week in ceremonies presided over by Maj. Gen. William E. Depuy, the commanding general.

Since then Chris has toured American bases in Korea and the Philippines before heading to Los Angeles via Hawaii. She plans to return to Vietnam early in 1967.

"THIS IS REALLY out of sight," said Chris when she accepted the honor of being adopted by the Big Red One. In the way out showgirl-ese of the go-go team that has made her the division's ideal doll, she added: "It's so cool, I'm in love with every one of these guys."

Then Depuy, in the fatherly way that generals have of looking after daughters of the division, immediately whirled her away in his helicopter for his morning tour of the battlefront.

The miniskirted charmer from West Palm Beach, Fla., recently at about twelve up to the Big Red One's famous motto: "No mission too difficult, no sacrifice too great; duty first."

She tramped out to the rifle emplacements, braving four charges of her ribbed white po-boy sweater, to chat with the boys in another bunker. ... blame, you expect her to come on flip and sassy; instead she comes on gentle and sincere and cuddly, more like the wholesome cheerleader from the high school back home than a jet set swinger.

Her kittenish costume suggests a Go-Go Girl out for kicks in a square world, but her husky voice, slightly breathless with excitement, communicates moonlight on the back porch, chocolate sundaes at the corner drug store and the girls they left behind.

CHRIS NOEL is an actress with several movies to her credit ("Get Yourself A Collete Girl"), but her rapport with the soldiers is ...

ASSOCIATED PRESS

I opened my daily radio show by saying Hi love, and these soldiers from Communications Section returned the favor when I visited them in Vietnam.

Sunny, one so true, I love you." But when when I sang it, I'd substitute soldiers names for "Sunny."

...Billy... ...One so true... ...I love you!"

Above Long Binh, January 2, 1968. Photo by Sp/4 Dick Freeman, 199th Infantry Brigade.

Below: Signing autographs for the troops. My honor!

Sgt. Doug Westney and Chris, Chu Lai, May 1967

140 / CHRIS NOEL-CONFESSIONS OF A PIN-UP GIRL

Opposite page
Visiting the 85th Evacuation Hospital, Ward 8, in Qui Nhon. Outside the hospital doors, it was all smiles and posing for pretty pictures.

Top of this page
Inside the doors lay the injury and pain of war. The Pentagon sent me to Vietnam to increase morale. Sometimes I went places that did not make for pretty pictures, like the field hospital seen in the photo above. As you can see, this picture was not cleared for publication.

Right:
Visiting Lcpl D. Moore in the 3rd Marine Amphibian Hospital, December 1967

Exiting the Fire Direction Center bunker

"Chris Sends Word to Charlie"

I SIGNED A BOMB on one of my trips to Vietnam. I wrote on it "To Charlie, Love Chris Noel." Charlie was the slang name our soldiers used to refer to the enemy. After I signed it, a soldier took it and loaded it into a Howitzer, then asked me if I wanted to fire the weapon off myself.

"Sure," I replied, "Why not?"

I pulled the lanyard, firing the live bomb I had just signed out of the howitzer. What a terrific explosion it made! It was all innocent enough, but as it turned out, not everyone thought so. Especially a certain French doctor. After I fired off the howitzer, oh boy did I get into trouble!

It was like a scene out of a movie. I was called to Saigon, and officially reprimanded by the Commander of AFVN (Armed Forces Vietnam Network). He told me some French doctor had contacted the White House, and lodged a formal complaint about what I had done, because, he said, "An American actress should not be allowed to fire heavy weaponry."

"It wasn't *my* idea!" I told him, "They *asked* me to fire that gun!"

But the Commander was in no mood to listen. He said that I was not to "endanger myself" by signing any more bombs, or firing off any more guns. Period!

Still, despite the minor international incident I had created, a photo of me shooting off that Howitzer appeared on the front page of newspapers around the world, including "Stars and Stripes," the official newspaper of the American military, with the caption *"Chris Sends Word To Charlie" (pictured on opposite page)*.

I hope a certain French doctor saw that headline!

Below:
U.S. Army Howitzer, the type of gun I fired off.

LBJ Clamps Lid on Book Discussion

AUSTIN, Tex. (UPI) — President Johnson refuses and has directed his staff to refuse to discuss any matters relating to the controversial "The Death of a President," book by William Manchester.

On the denying of "attributions" in a Newsweek magazine article which quoted Johnson as differing sharply with accounts of events following the assassination of President John F. Kennedy, Press Secretary George Christian said:

"The President has granted no interviews to anyone, including Mr. Manchester, and has asked his staff to refrain from discussing the subject—the entire subject of the book."

"He did not talk to Newsweek," Christian said. "And I'll not discuss the various attributions credited to so-called friends and alleged intimates except to say that I believe them to be inaccurate and untrue."

A section of the Manchester book reportedly tells of Mrs. Kennedy's shock at finding Johnson and his party already in command aboard the presidential plane, Air Force One, by the time Kennedy's body was borne aboard in a coffin.

The magazine says Johnson recalls the Secret Service wanted to put him aboard Air Force One because of its superior communications gear and to place the Kennedy coffin on the vice presidential
(Continued on Back Page, Col. 5)

PACIFIC STARS AND STRIPES

AN AUTHORIZED PUBLICATION OF THE ARMED FORCES IN THE FAR EAST

FIVE-STAR EDITION

10¢ DAILY
15¢ WITH SUPPLEMENTS

Vol. 22, No. 361   Wednesday, Dec. 28, 1966

Battle at Bong Son
REDS HIT CAV. UNIT

SAIGON (AP) — Troops of the U.S. 1st Air Cav. Div. were attacked early Tuesday by a strong communist force 300 miles north of Saigon.

It was the first major ground action since the end of the 48-hour Christmas truce.

U.S. spokesmen said there was no immediate word on casualties for either side. The battle was located in the battle-scarred Bong Son area near the South China Sea.

At one point during the communist attack on the Cavalrymen, communication with the U.S. forces was lost.

In the air war, American B-52s bombed about 60 miles northwest of Cam Ranh Bay Tuesday. The target was said to
(Continued on Back Page, Col. 1)

Death Calls Nick The Greek

LOS ANGELES (UPI) — Nick the Greek Dandolos, who claimed to have won and lost over $500 million in a half-century career as a gambler, died Christmas night at Mt. Sinai Hospital.

Dandolos, the philosophical gambler known as the "Aristotle of the don't pass line," died of massive internal bleeding.
(Continued on Back Page, Col. 3)

Glad Tidings From Russ Ship

SAIGON (AP) — The captain of the U.S. Seventh Fleet tug Arikara broke a cold war chill over Christmas by flashing a holiday greeting to the Russian trawler Bacerograph in the gulf of Tonkin.

Within seconds, Lt. C. E. Stith received a reply from the Soviet ship.

"Happy Christmas, best congratulations and wishes in '67. Let it be a year of peace. Good Luck."

Chris Sends Word to Charlie

Disc jockey Chris Noel, the U.S. answer to Hanoi Hannah, pulls the lanyard on a 105mm howitzer at a 5d Brigade, First Inf. Div., base 25 miles north of Saigon. Troops were firing at a suspected Viet Cong concentration. (AP Radiophoto)

Uncle Found to Claim Body of Veteran

SAN FRANCISCO (AP) — The body of Army Sgt. Richard Campos, which had lain unclaimed for two weeks at the Oakland (Cal.) Army Terminal, was claimed Monday by his uncle.

"6th Army headquarters at Presidio here said John Campos, a field hand from Marysville, Cal., presented baptismal proof of his relationship. He also provided the Army with leads to other relatives.

"We have forwarded all the proof of kinship on to Washington," an Army spokesman said. "The decision on whether to release Sgt. Campos' body will be made at the Pentagon."

When the uncle was discovered Sunday by a Sacramento (Cal.) Union reporter in a shabby hotel room in Sacramento, he was unaware of the nationwide search for his nephew's relatives. He had not seen Richard since he was 12 years old.

With representatives of Mexican-American groups from Sacramento, Campos drove to San Francisco Monday to claim the body. Publicity about the unclaimed body of the orphan, who was killed Dec. 6 on patrol in Vietnam, had stirred nationwide interest.

Individuals, private groups and veterans organizations had offered to bury the 26-year-old sergeant, but the Army had declined all offers, explaining the body could be released only to a blood or legal relative.

(The Army was reported searching in Japan and Korea for a girl Campos told friends he married, UPI said. Friends said Campos told them he married while in Korea.)

Both state and San Francisco lawmakers Monday said they would ask the legislature and the city to build a memorial to Campos. Assemblyman Willie Brown said he will offer a resolution on the first day of the new legislative session next Monday detailing Campos' life.

Democratic U.S. Rep. Philip Burton expressed concern about the recognition for the young man's service to his country.

Sgt. Campos was born at Carbondale, Cal. He was orphaned in 1942 when his 10-year-old mother died of tuberculosis. He then lived with an aunt, Maria Campos in San Francisco, until authorities took him away and placed him in a series of foster homes. He joined the Army at the age of 17.

Because my name sounded like Christmas, and I visited Vietnam several times during that holiday, sometimes I was called Miss Christmas.

Marvel Comics The Nam #23 Oct. 1988, cover by Pepe Moreno, featured me in a special story that was written by Doug Murray, penciled by Wayne Vansant, and edited by Larry Hama -- all veterans of the Vietnam War.

Performing with Bob Hope

APPEARING IN Bob Hope's USO show in Vietnam on Christmas Day was one of the highlights of my career. Bob was a legend. In 1996, Congress declared him to be the "first and only honorary veteran of the United States armed forces."

He appeared in or hosted more than 200 USO shows, and I'm thrilled to have appeared in one of them — even though it wasn't originally planned at all! Here's how it happened.

I was touring Vietnam during Christmas 1966 when my military escort told me that Bob Hope would be performing in nearby Cu Chi, a village famous for its vast network of underground tunnels. My escort asked me if I wanted to appear in Mr. Hope's show, and I jumped at the

CHRIS NOEL VISIT TO VIETNAM — Drawing the most applause of the show, Chris appears with Bob Hope at Cu Chi, the home of the 25th Infantry Division, 25 December 1966.

chance. I wasn't very far away, so the army sent a helicopter to pick me up.

I was flown to Camp Eagle, where I met Bob in the mess tent. I couldn't believe I was actually in Vietnam with Bob Hope — and on Christmas Day!

We performed in an outdoor auditorium called the Eagle Entertainment Bowl. When Bob introduced me, he said, "North Vietnam has Hanoi Hanna, so our government found a girl who I'm sure will top her by a long shot, because she's one of our most beautiful gals. Chris Noel — Miss Christmas — right here."

When I came onstage, and Bob stared at my mini-skirt. "This is what they're wearing in the States," I told him in a sexy voice, "in case you're wondering."

"I'm glad you said that," Bob cracked, "Because I thought something had shrunk."

For my act, I read a funny, Vietnamized version of *The Night Before Christmas*. I was thrilled that everyone, especially Bob, seemed to love it. What a day!

PHOTO: DR. JAMES HUGHES

Chris Noel & Bob Hope performing in Vietnam

CONFESSIONS OF A PIN-UP GIRL - CHRIS NOEL / 151

PART FOUR
Hollywood Ending

IN THE SPRING OF 1968, my mentor, the late, great Martha Raye, introduced me to a soft-spoken man who offered to show me around Camp Goodman, in Vietnam. I was quite impressed by this young lieutenant, a Green Beret.

His name was Clyde Berkeley Herrington, but everyone called him "Ty." We strolled around Camp Goodman together, and I found myself enjoying his company quite a bit.

I'd dated some of Hollywood's hottest men, but Ty was different. He wasn't "Hollywood" at all. I was reminded of Frank Sinatra and all his friends being fascinated with Mia Farrow because she was "different." Now I knew how they felt!

Ty took me to his living quarters and we talked. He was sensitive and protective. I also thought he was great looking, and acted like a real southern gentleman. We began seeing each other regularly.

A few months later, Ty told me, "Come on Chris, I've got a surprise for you. We're going to Cambodia."

"Oh Ty, we're not supposed to do that. We could get shot! But... oh well, let's go anyway."

We went by helicopter, just the two of us and the pilot. While we watched a spectacular sunset from the air, Ty turned to me and asked, "Will you marry me?"

I yelled my answer to Ty above the noise of the chopper, "Yes!"

We got married shortly after that, in the Miami home of my matron of honor, Patty Olsen Rautbord. During our honeymoon we attended President Nixon's inaugural ball.

Everything was going great. I had no idea that in a year's time, a horrific tragedy would suddenly tear my entire life apart.

Mr. and Mrs. Ty Herrington at President-Elect Richard Nixon's Inaugural Ball, January 20, 1969

saddened than those thousands of GI's around the world who knew Chris through her daily Armed Forces Radio Show.

To these men, Chris was their girl friend, their mom and sweetheart, their link with home while they were so very far away. Many of them had met her during one of her frequent trips to mili-

Husband takes his own life

Chris took on the job with Armed Forces Radio in an attempt to offset the propaganda effects of Hanoi Hannah.

When they had to be separated for her birthday, Ty arranged to surprise her with a cake and party on her return

CEASE FIRE
Director: David Nutter
Studio: ELF/Double Helix Films
Screenplay by: George Fernandez
Release date: October 18, 1985
Cast: Don Johnson, Lisa Blount, Robert F. Lyons, Chris Noel
Length: 97 minutes, color
Trivia: First movie to deal with "Post Traumatic Stress Syndrome" among Vietnam veterans

Cease Fire

ART IMITATED LIFE when I got a part in the Vietnam movie "Cease Fire," starring Don Johnson (*Miami Vice*).

This movie was definitely not a Rambo-style shoot-em-up, it was a thoughtful and insightful look at the plight of troubled Vietnam veterans in post-war America.

In the film, I played a vet's wife who becomes a widow as a result of his suicide — a story echoing my own real life.

About a year after we got married, my husband Ty shot himself, leaving me in a state of shock and devastation from which I have never fully recovered, even after remarrying and the passage of many, many years.

In "Cease Fire," I join other women affected by the Vietnam war, and we bear our souls during a gut-wrenching group therapy session.

My performance drew some of the best reviews of my career. *Variety* said "Chris Noel shines," and movie critic Joni Siani said, "Chris Noel gives an Academy Award performance."

We filmed my big scene in just one take, and when I finished speaking the cast and crew unexpectedly burst into applause. They all knew what I had been through personally, and how close to home the scene hit for me.

"Thank you all so much," I told them with a laugh. "And thank God we got it in one take!"

"CEASE FIRE"

"He never hit me! I mean, there was never anything like that. My husband and I really tried. At least I think we did. It sure hasn't been easy. Then again, maybe it's not supposed to be. But I *know* that I tried. And I still don't understand what's happening."

"I get so tired of what's going on. I get so tired of watching him destroy all the wonderful things about him that I love so much. And my kid? He idolizes him. And I can see the pain in his eyes. I know that he knows... I know that he knows his father is crazy."

"I am so tired of it. I am so tired of what's going on. I don't know if we're going to get back together again. And sometimes I don't really care. *I am so tired of Vietnam!*"

--Chris Noel, Cease Fire
SCREENWRITER: GEORGE FERNANDEZ

As his wife, former 1960s starlet Chris Noel ("Soldier In The Rain," "The Glory Stompers") shines in a heartfelt monolog delivered at a group session for veterans' wives. *Variety*, July 10, 1985

Vetsville Cease Fire House

Vetsville is dedicated to sheltering America's homeless veterans. Find us at ceasefirehouse.org

MY LIFE was shattered. More than anything else, I wanted to help others like myself — people who had been damaged, either physically or mentally, by the Vietnam War. The former pin-up girl became a veteran's advocate.

I founded a non-profit charity dedicated to providing food, shelter and care for America's indigent veterans. Inspired by the name of my 1985 film, my charity was christened "Vetsville Cease Fire House."

Founded in Florida in February 1993, Vetsville has helped *thousands* of Vietnam veterans reclaim their lives with pride and dignity. We couldn't operate without my dear friend Don Marlow, who has been managing Cease Fire House for many years.

Why so many American veterans are homeless? It's because when people join the military, the Government feeds, clothes, houses and trains them for specific jobs.

Then, when they leave the service, they suddenly have to learn how to survive back in the civilian world. Most are able to cope, with the help of family and friends— but not everyone is blessed with having family and friends. Some people seem to fall through the holes in our "safety nets," and can't make it on their own. They need help. Vetsville's goal is to *give* them that help.

CHRIS NOEL DURING TOUR OF VIETNAM
Hollywood no longer a driving force for her

By Harry V. Martin

The suffering, sadness, anger and bitterness she saw in a visit to an Army hospital changed her life - forever. She transformed her Hollywood career into helping the veterans of war.

This week Chris Noel is spending the week at the Moving Wall display at the Veterans Home in Yountville. She assisted in the opening ceremonies Sunday night at the Wall - a solemn occasion honoring the fallen of America's wars. Chris was a successful performer on radio and in motion pictures, co-starring with such illuminaries as Steve McQueen, Elvis Presley, Richard Chamberlain, Don Johnson, Nancy Sinatra, Chad Everett, Frankie Avalon, Ed Byrnes and John Saxon. She also appeared on television in the ABC Mystery Movie, China Beach, Chips, Bewitched, Dr. Kildaire, Hollywood Palace, Perry Mason, My Three Sons and Bob Hope Presents.

Chris had the number one daily radio series on Armed Forces Radio - "A Date with Chris" for five years, worldwide. Today, Chris is the founder of three Florida shelters for disabled and homeless American veterans. She uses her talent to raise funds, obtain grants to feed and house the former fighting men of this nation who have fallen on hard times.

Her life changed on Christmas Day 1965 when, while under contract to MGM, she visited Letterman Hospital in the San Francisco Presidio. She visited the gangrene ward. She immediately noticed the bitterness, the hurt and anger, the depression of the men in that ward - their bodies

Rolling Thunder Motorcycle Rally

Every year, an estimated half-million participants ride into the nation's capital to bring awareness to the plight of prisoners of war (POW) and to those missing in action (MIA). The Rolling Thunder Memorial Day weekend event -- begun in 1987 -- has since evolved into a demonstration of patriotism and respect for soldiers and veterans from all wars.

ROLLING THUNDER RUN COMMANDER
ARTIE MULLER

VIETNAM WAR ICONS

JON VOIGHT, "COMING HOME"

BRUCE SPRINGSTEEN, "BORN IN THE USA"

ADRIAN CRONAUER, "GOOD MORNING VIETNAM"

MARTIN SHEEN, "APOCALYPSE NOW"

RON KOVIK, "BORN OF THE 4th of JULY"

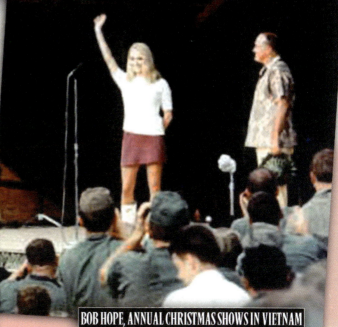
BOB HOPE, ANNUAL CHRISTMAS SHOWS IN VIETNAM

LZ LAMBEAU WELCOME HOME
Network: Wisconsin Public TV
Air date: May 22, 2010
Length: 108 minutes, color
Honors: Emmy Award Winner, Outstanding Achievement for Special Event Programming

LZ Lambeau Welcome Home

ON May 22, 2010, I was honored to be master of ceremonies for "Landing Zone Lambeau Welcome Home," a three-day extravaganza.

About 70,000 people attended the event, which was the state of Wisconsin's long-overdue recognition of its Vietnam veterans, offering them the warm, public welcome home that most never received.

"Welcome Home" was the subject of an award-winning documentary, created by Wisconsin Public Television. The show won an Emmy Award for Outstanding Achievement for Special Event Programming.

I was so thrilled to be part of this event, and when I found out it had won an Emmy Award, I was overjoyed.

Anything that reminds the public of our Vietnam veterans makes me happy, and to me, the recognition of this special event meant the realization of a life-long dream.

Ever since I was a little girl growing up in West Palm Beach, Florida, I wanted to be famous. But I learned that the real blessing of being "famous" is being able to *use* your fame to help other people, especially the brave military men and women who once fought for *all of us*.

These words were scribbled by a Marine on a bunker wall in Khe Sanh: "For those who have fought for it, freedom has a flavor the protected will never know."

"LZ LAMBEAU WELCOME HOME"

CHRIS NOEL FILMOGRAPHY

SOLDIER IN THE RAIN
Chris as Frances McCoy
United Artists
Released November 27, 1963

HONEYMOON HOTEL
Chris as Nancy Penrose
Metro-Goldwyn-Mayer
Released June 3, 1964

DIARY OF A BACHELOR
Chris as Carol
American International
Released November 27, 1964

GET YOURSELF A COLLEGE GIRL
Chris as Sue Ann
Metro-Goldwyn-Mayer
Released December 18, 1964

LOOKING FOR LOVE
Chris as Flo
Metro-Goldwyn-Mayer
Released November 27, 1964

GIRL HAPPY
Chris as Betsy
Metro-Goldwyn-Mayer
Released April 7, 1965

JOY IN THE MORNING
Chris as Mary Ellen Kincaid
Metro-Goldwyn-Mayer
Released May 5, 1965

BEACH BALL
Chris as Susan Collins
American International
Released September 29, 1965

WILD, WILD WINTER
Chris as Susan
American International
Released January 5, 1966

THE GLORY STOMPERS
Chris as Chris
American International
Released January 1968

FOR SINGLES ONLY
Chris as Lily
Columbia
Released June 5.1968

THE TORMENTORS aka TERMINATORS
Chris as Eve
Associated Screen Artists
Released 1971

WILD TIMES
Chris as Dolly
Made for TV movie
Aired January 24, 1980

DETOUR TO TERROR
Chris as Peggy Cameron
Made for TV movie
Aired February 22, 1980

CEASE FIRE
Chris as Wendy
ELF/Double Helix Films
Released October 18, 1985

BLONDE BOMBSHELL THE CHRIS NOEL STORY
Biography documentary
Released July 4, 2004

SOLDIER IN THE RAIN

GIRL HAPPY

JOY IN THE MORNING

BEACH BALL

THE GLORY STOMPERS

CEASE FIRE

168 / CONFESSIONS OF A PIN-UP GIRL by CHRIS NOEL

CHRIS NOEL TV APPEARANCES

The Red Skelton Hour
(CBS- 1962)

Jan Murray's Charge Account
Game show co-hostess
(NBC- 1962)

The Edge of Night
(CBS- 1962)

The Steve Allen Show
(NBC- November 28, 1963)

The Eleventh Hour
"Trying To Keep Alive Until Next Tuesday"
(NBC- April 17, 1963)

United States Steel Hour
(ABC-1963)

The Hollywood Deb Star Ball
(ABC- December 28, 1963)

Hollywood and the Stars
"Teenage Idols" w/ Fabian
(NBC- January 20, 1964)

The Regis Philbin Show
(NBC- June 6, 1964)

The Lieutenant
Seven Episodes
(NBC- September 14, 1963 - April 18, 1964)

Bewitched
"Love is Blind"
(ABC- December 10, 1964)

Dr. Kildare
(NBC- 1965)

Play Your Hunch
(CBS- May 1965)

The Smothers Brothers
"I Wouldn't Miss My Own Funeral For Anything"
(CBS- November 5, 1965)

American Bandstand
(ABC- February 27, 1965)

Burke's Law
Two episodes:
"Who Killed Mr. Colby in Ladies' Lingerie?"
(ABC-March 3, 1965)

"Who Killed the Grand Piano?"
(ABC-April 28, 1965)

Legal Eagle aka The Lawyer
Unsold Pilot (1965)

Perry Mason
"The Case of the Silent Six"
(November 21, 1965)

(Continued on next page)

THE LIEUTENANT

LEGAL EAGLE

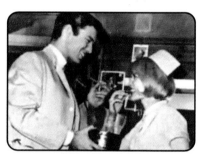
DR. KILDARE

TEENAGE IDOLS

PERRY MASON

170 / CONFESSIONS OF A PIN-UP GIRL by CHRIS NOEL

More CHRIS NOEL TV APPEARANCES

O.K. Crackerby
"Crackerby and The Cuckoo Game"
(ABC- December 9, 1965)

My Three Sons
"Marriage and Stuff"
(CBS- December 10, 1965)

My Mother the Car
"Many Happy No-Returns"
(NBC- Dec. 21, 1965)

Pistols 'n' Petticoats
Unaired pilot
(CBS- 1966)

Love on a Rooftop
Episode title unknown
(ABC- 1966)

Vacation Playhouse: The Good Old Days
Series Pilot
(CBS- July 11, 1966)

Occasional Wife
"Series Pilot,"
  (NBC- September 13, 1966)
"Danger, Woman at Work,"
  (NBC- November 1, 1966)
"Peter by Moonlight,"
  (NBC- December 27, 1966)

Bob Hope Comedy Hour
Variety show
(NBC- November 16, 1966)

The Bob Hope Show
(NBC- January 18, 1967)

The Pat Boone Show
(NBC- February 14/15, 1967)

The Tonight Show with Johnny Carson
(NBC- 1965, 1967)

Dream Girl
(ABC- February 24, 1967)

The Mini-Skirt Rebellion
Television Special
(ABC- February 28, 1967)

The Dating Game
Celebrity contestant
(ABC- March 25, 1967)

The Merv Griffin Show
(NBC- 1967)

What's My Line?
(CBS- February 5, 1967)

The Hollywood Palace
(ABC- February 25, 1967)

Password
Chris vs. Roger Smith
(CBS- March 27-31, 1967)

The Joey Bishop Show
(ABC- 1968)

(Continued on next page)

MY THREE SONS

MY MOTHER THE CAR

OCCASIONAL WIFE

PASSWORD

BOB HOPE SPECIAL

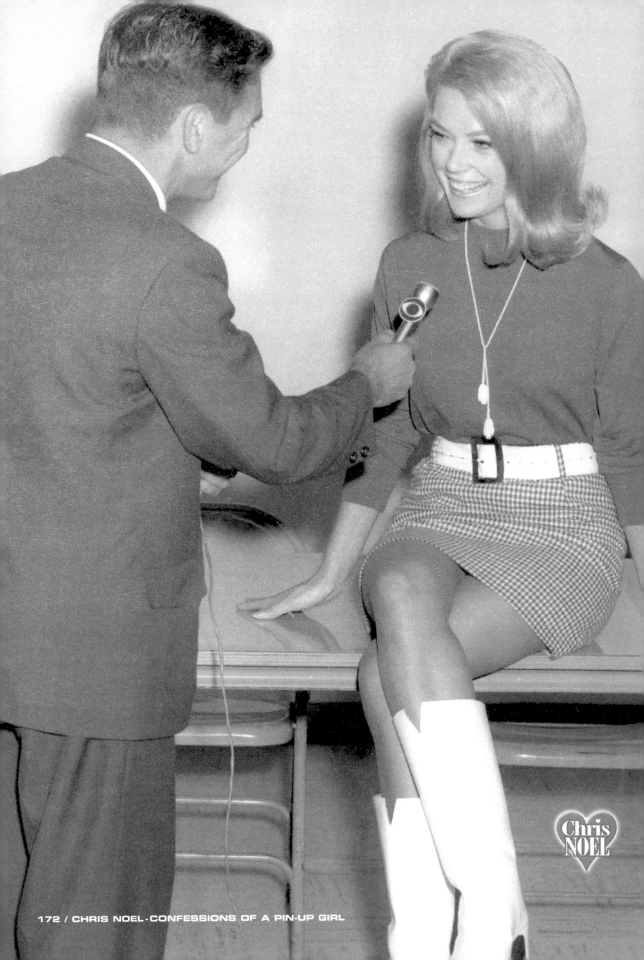

Even more CHRIS NOEL TV APPEARANCES

Pat Boone in Hollywood
Talk show guest
(SYNDICATED- Jan.1, 1968)

Pat Boone Show
(NBC- January 31,1968)

The Mike Douglas Show
(SYNDICATED- Aug. 13, 1968)

The Donald O'Connor Show
(SYNDICATED- January 10, 1969)

The Skitch Henderson Show
(SYNDICATED- January 28, 1969)

Hans Holzer's Haunted
Exploring the supernatural (1972)

Going Platinum
Chris interviews Charley Pride
(SHOWTIME- October 11, 1980)

The PTL Club
Chris sings "Forgotten Man"
(PTL SATELLITE NETWORK- 1980)

CHiPs
"11-99: Officer Needs Help"
(NBC- January 18, 1981)

Entertainment Tonight
"Cease Fire Premiere Party"
(SYNDICATED- 1985)

Entertainment Tonight
"Pin-Up Girls"
(SYNDICATED- 1985)

China Beach
Chris plays herself
"Vets"
(ABC- March 15, 1989)

Burt Reynolds as B.L. Stryker
"Blues for Buder"
(ABC- May 15, 1989)

Welcome Home Heroes
(HBO- March 31, 1991)

Vietnam: Soldier's Story
"Women At War"
(TLC- February 7, 2000)

CBS Evening News with Dan Rather
Feature story
(CBS- January 2001)

The Definitive Elvis
"The Hollywood Years"
Part Two
(DVD BOX SET- 2002)

Rolling Thunder Rally
Annual event in Washington, DC
(C-SPAN- 2003-present)

LZ Lambeau Welcome Home
(PBS- May 22, 2010)
EMMY AWARD WINNER
Outstanding Achievement for Special Event Programming

THE DEFINITIVE ELVIS

FORGOTTEN MAN

VIETNAM: WOMEN AT WAR

ENTERTAINMENT TONIGHT

CBS EVENING NEWS

174 / CONFESSIONS OF A PIN-UP GIRL by CHRIS NOEL

CHRIS NOEL IN VIETNAM

FIRST TOUR - DECEMBER 1966
- Eleven-day tour of U.S. bases and hospitals in Vietnam
- Mini-skirt almost causes tank accident at Lai Khe
- Sings for the Big Red One (1st Infantry Division)
- Fires howitzer "illegally," gets reprimand from Colonel
- Surveys An Khe valley from atop Hong Kong mountain
- Visits troops in Pleiko, Da Nang, Qui Nhon, and Saigon
- Performs with Bob Hope at Cu Chi on Christmas Day

SECOND TOUR - JANUARY 1967
- Ten-day tour of U.S. bases and hospitals in Vietnam
- Talk with soldiers in remote sandbag bunkers
- In a scene out of a beach party movie, Chris plays a rock record and dances with a cook on top of a mess hall table
- "Adopted" by the Big Red One (1st Infantry Div.)

THIRD TOUR - MAY 1967
- Attends soldiers run at Chu Lai in Dung Quat Bay
- Mini-skirt causes raging controversy in Saigon
- Visits military hospitals, talks with wounded soldiers

FOURTH TOUR - DECEMBER 1967
- Performs on USS Ticonderoga in Gulf of Tonkin, singing on deck for hundreds of crew members
- Named "Tico Tigress" by crew of USS Ticonderoga
- Visits wounded Marines in 3rd Marine Amph. Hospital

FIFTH TOUR - JANUARY 1968
- Sings "Sunny" and more for 2nd BN/3rd Inf, 199th Infantry Brigade, Army Cmd. HQ, Long Binh, Vietnam
- Tours 199th Infantry Brigade Fire Support Base
- Visits hospitals and aid stations, talks with patients

SIXTH TOUR - MAY 1968
- Visits troops in Korea, sings "Feelin' Groovy" and more
- Sings for U.S. troops stationed in Thailand
- Visits 11th Infantry Brigade at Duc Pho, Vietnam
- Entertains 2nd Infantry Division troops in Vietnam

SEVENTH TOUR - DECEMBER 1968
- "Miss Christmas" makes her final Christmas trip to Vietnam, to entertain the troops
- Visits 85th Evacuation Hospital in Qui Nhon, Vietnam

EIGHTH TOUR - JUNE 1969
(Complete itinerary on next page)

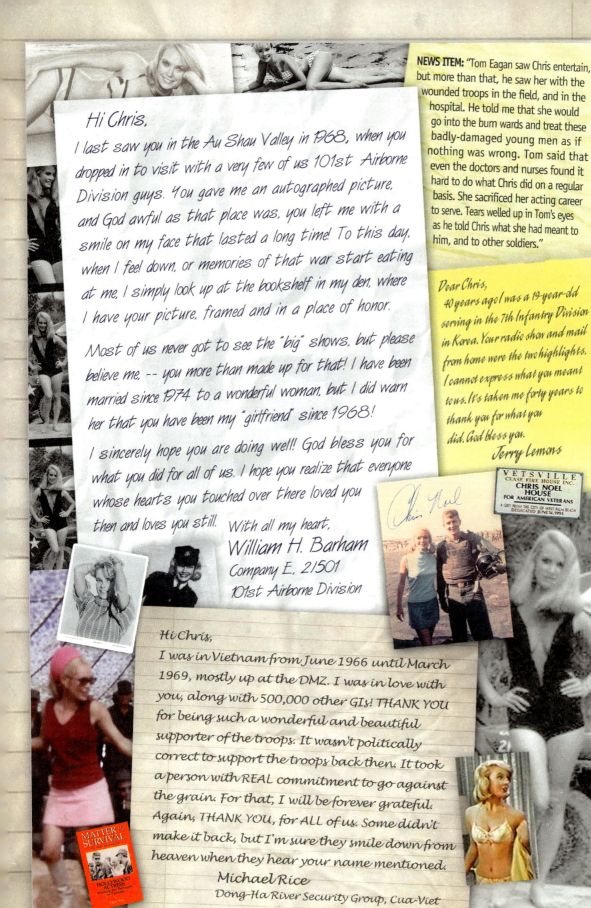

NEWS ITEM: "Tom Eagan saw Chris entertain, but more than that, he saw her with the wounded troops in the field, and in the hospital. He told me that she would go into the burn wards and treat these badly-damaged young men as if nothing was wrong. Tom said that even the doctors and nurses found it hard to do what Chris did on a regular basis. She sacrificed her acting career to serve. Tears welled up in Tom's eyes as he told Chris what she had meant to him, and to other soldiers."

Hi Chris,

I last saw you in the Au Shau Valley in 1968, when you dropped in to visit with a very few of us 101st Airborne Division guys. You gave me an autographed picture, and God awful as that place was, you left me with a smile on my face that lasted a long time! To this day, when I feel down, or memories of that war start eating at me, I simply look up at the bookshelf in my den, where I have your picture, framed and in a place of honor.

Most of us never got to see the "big" shows, but please believe me, -- you more than made up for that! I have been married since 1974 to a wonderful woman, but I did warn her that you have been my "girlfriend" since 1968!

I sincerely hope you are doing well!! God bless you for what you did for all of us. I hope you realize that everyone whose hearts you touched over there loved you then and loves you still.

With all my heart,
William H. Barham
Company E, 21501
101st Airborne Division

Dear Chris,

40 years ago I was a 19-year-old serving in the 7th Infantry Division in Korea. Your radio show and mail from home were the two highlights. I cannot express what you meant to us. It's taken me forty years to thank you for what you did. God bless you.

Jerry Lemons

Hi Chris,

I was in Vietnam from June 1966 until March 1969, mostly up at the DMZ. I was in love with you, along with 500,000 other GIs! THANK YOU for being such a wonderful and beautiful supporter of the troops. It wasn't politically correct to support the troops back then. It took a person with REAL commitment to go against the grain. For that, I will be forever grateful. Again, THANK YOU, for ALL of us. Some didn't make it back, but I'm sure they smile down from heaven when they hear your name mentioned.

Michael Rice
Dong-Ha River Security Group, Cua-Viet

REPRODUCED AT THE NATIONAL ARCHIVES

ARMED FORCES PROFESSIONAL ENTERTAINMENT
CONSOLIDATED ATTENDANCE AND FINAL ITINERARY REPORT

NOTE: TO BE COMPLETED IN 6 COPIES WITHIN 5 WORK DAYS AFTER THE UNIT HAS DEPARTED AND FORWARDED TO OFFICE OF THE PACOM ENTERTAINMENT COORDINATOR, APO 96323

UNIT NAME AND NUMBER: **CHRIS NOEL SHOW**
DATE OF ARRIVAL: **19 June 1969**
ARRIVING FLIGHT NO.: **188**

DATE OF PERFORMANCE	SITE AND LOCATION OF PERFORMANCE (e.g. Post Theater, Camp and APO)	LENGTH OF SHOW	TVL	TYPE OF PERFORMANCE FACILITY	NUMBER OF ATTENDEES	USING SERVICE (e.g. USN, USMC, USAF, USA)
20 Jun 69	3RD FIELD HOSPITAL	120	40	N/A		
21 Jun 69	24TH EVAC HOSPITAL	90	20	N/A	250	ARMY
21 Jun 69	ARTY BTRY	60	20	N/A	200	USA
21 Jun 69	92RD EVAC HOSPITAL	120	20	N/A	40	USA
21 Jun 69	79TH MAINT BN	60	20	N/A	250	USA
22 Jun 69	LZ DEBBIE	60	10	N/A	500	USA
22 Jun 69	LZ ENGLISH	60	10	N/A	200	USA
22 Jun 69	LZ LOW BOY	120	30	N/A	300	USA
23 Jun 69	67 EVAC HOSPITAL	120	15	N/A	200	USA
23 Jun 69	TAM QUAN MACV TEAM 42	60	90	N/A	200	USA
23 Jun 69	THU MY MACV TEAM 42	120	30	N/A	50	USA
24 Jun 69	FIRE BASE SPT GROUP	120	30	N/A	100	USA
24 Jun 69	4TH INF DIV BASE CAMP	120	10	N/A	200	USA
25 Jun 69	FSB BRONCO	120	45	N/A	350	USA
25 Jun 69	FSB GOLDIE	120	20	N/A	500	USA
25 Jun 69	FSB DOTTIE	120	15	N/A	200	USA
26 Jun 69	USS FWO JI A	120	30	N/A	200	USA
26 Jun 69	USS CLEVELAND	120	15	N/A	650	USN
27 Jun 69	FSB ROY	60	15	N/A	800	USN
27 Jun 69	FSB BIRMINGHAM	45	15	N/A	50	USA
27 Jun 69	FSB RAKKASAN	45	30	N/A	250	USA
27 Jun 69	FSB BLAZE	45	30	N/A	100	USA
27 Jun 69	FSB BASTOGNE	30	15	N/A	150	USA
28 Jun 69	BINH THUY AFB	15	15	N/A	50	USA
29 Jun 69	MACV TEAM 50	120		N/A	300	USAF
29 Jun 69	MACV TEAM 97	120	210	N/A	100	USA
29 Jun 69	MACV TEAM 84	90	15	N/A	50	USA
30 Jun 69	29 EVAC HOSPITAL	120	30	N/A	150	USA
		120	15	N/A	200	USA

Dear Chris-
I love you.
I love you.
I love you.
I love you.
You are what we were fighting for in 'Nam. Thanks for being our badly-needed pin-up gal and for all the work you still do. Hollyweird really lost out by not appreciating you enough. WE DO. If my wife croaks, will you let me go out with you?

Love Larry,
Now an old fat Marine

Dear Chris,
You probably don't remember me, but we had an intimate time together in Danang. I was escorting you on your visit to the AFRTS TV station on Monkey Mountain. It was a real crappy night with rain, and the road going back to the billets was muddy. As luck would have it, a truck slipped off in a ditch, creating a lineup of vehicles on the road. Our pickup was right in the middle. The MP's came around and told everyone to turn off their lights because there were some snipers in the area. One of our soldiers accidently discharged his weapon, causing widespread panic. I pulled you down in the front seat and covered you so you wouldn't get hit. My name is Dave Hill, I was a Petty Officer First Class in the Navy at the time and assigned on temporary duty with the AFRTS engineering unit in Saigon. They sent me to Danang with you. Thought you might enjoy recalling my memorable occasion with you.

Love always, Dave Hill

Hi Chris
I served with the 25th ID in CuChi from 66-67 and with the 173rd Assault Helicopter Co in Lai Khe leaving following Tet in 68. I will always remember the comfort your voice gave us when we listened to you on AFRVN.
Thank you so much for everything you did to keep us cheered up when we faced such terrible conditions. You are the best! —Eddie Lowenstein

---

Chris, I was in Vietnam from March 71- Jan 72 and I had a pin-up of you. I just wanted to tell you that I looked at it many times (as did a lot of guys in my unit) remembering that somewhere back home "in the world" a girl just like you was waiting for me. My dear, sweet lady, you truely were the inspiration for many guys just like me to look forward to coming home. God bless you in all you do for the Vets and trust me, you have been and always will be in my heart, thoughts, and prayers.
—Terry Rook Sr.

Acknowledgments
Thank you for your love and support

My parents, Louise and David Botz, my sister Trudie and her husband John Saturno; as well as Armed Forces Radio and Television Service; Dr. Jose Alfonso; Kevin Baldwin; Lynne Baldwin; Mike Bartlett; Blain Baur; Christina Baroque; Dr. Kenneth Beer; Dr. Jamie Bensimon; Clifton Berry; John and Jacquie Bray; Rod Burk; Don Bush; Paulette Carlson; Ginny and Mike Carroll; Adolph Caso; Tom Corey; Bryant and Donna Culpepper; Arnie Everson; Tom Eggers; Elvis Presley Enterprises, Inc.; Donna of Famous Faces; Pam and Harry Flynn; Patty Rautbord Frankel; Richard Fielden; Gary Franks; Buddy Galon; Claudia Gary; Mary Green; Thomas Girvin; Graceland; Wes Gunty; Phyllis and Mike Haggerty; Bill Hancock; Doug Heatherly; Tom Hodges; Bruce Irvine; Lori Jacobson; Jack Jones; Jeff Jon; Barbara Katz; Jeff Keane; Kathy Kersh; Paul Kruger; Dan Kruger; Cathi Lechareas; Victoria Lesser, Kat Litrenta; MGM; Dr. Edward Mallen; Don Marlowe; Shad Meshad; Janet Metz; Reid Moore; Artie and Elaine Muller; Nam Knights Motorcycle Club; Hugh O'Brian; Eileen O'Neil; Nick Papayani; Arthur Patrick; Daniel Pereira; GySgt. Will Price, USMC; Sidney and Paul Revere and the Raiders; Michael Rhodes; Al Tresconi at MGM; Tracy Reiner; David Riker; David Rollings, Esq.; Barbara Lee Rowe; Rolling Thunder, Jeff Rose; Pat Sajak; Rick Sapphire; Gina Saturno; Marlo Dahl; Michael Saturno; Tony Schebell; Elliot Shaw, Nancy Sinatra; Betty Jo Sheely; Ted Spock; Mary Taylor; Marshall Terrill; George Martin Tragona; Minh and Mike Tran; Paul Truczinskas; Dr. Daniel Tucker; Judy Upton; Mark Vega; The Vietnam Veterans of America; Peggy Watford; Robbie Wilde; Trudie Marie Wilde; Ted Witzer; David Yarosh; Kim and Dr. Keith Yu; Dr. Jerry Zupnik; and all the reporters, photographers, directors, producers, actors, crew members, and military personnel who have worked with me over the years. And a special kiss from Chris to all my fans!

Made in the USA
Lexington, KY
03 January 2013